ECOCRITICISM AND ENVIRONMENTAL PRAXIS

ECOCRITICISM
AND ENVIRONMENTAL
PRAXIS

edited by

SHIVANI JHA

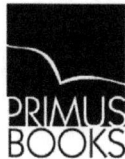

PRIMUS
BOOKS

PRIMUS BOOKS

An imprint of Ratna Sagar P. Ltd.

Virat Bhavan
Mukherjee Nagar Commercial Complex
Delhi 110 009

Offices at

CHENNAI   LUCKNOW

AGRA   AHMEDABAD   BANGALORE   COIMBATORE
DEHRADUN   GUWAHATI   HYDERABAD   JAIPUR   JALANDHAR
KANPUR   KOCHI   KOLKATA   MADURAI   MUMBAI
PATNA   RANCHI   VARANASI

First published 2017

ISBN: 978-93-84092-23-8 (hardback)
ISBN: 978-93-84092-24-5 (POD)
ISBN: 978-93-84092-25-2 (e-book)

PUBLISHED BY PRIMUS BOOKS

Laser typeset by Guru Typograph Technology
Crossings Republic, Ghaziabad 201 009

Printed and bound in India by Replika Press Pvt. Ltd.

Contents

Preface

HAD HUMAN HABITATION been confined to floating spaceships, disconnected from the land, impervious to its surroundings, then perhaps this book would have been superfluous. But, such is not the case. Being a planetary community, humans are hugely affected by the changes in the environment. The extent of these changes and the magnitude of their impact on humans have prompted scientists to declare the modern times as the age of the anthropocene. It is, thus, an age characterized by anthropogenic interventions where man has revamped the environment like individually owned, private condominiums, with devastating though unintended consequences.

In his essay 'The Anthropocene Mass Extinction: An Emerging Curriculum Theme for Science Educators', Ron Wagler conveys the magnitude of the damage to the environment incurred so far and warns of its intensifying further in future for want of the necessary ameliyoratory measures. Wagler cites studies pertaining to acceleration in the global species extinction rate that find it to be 100 to 10,000 times Earth's historical geological background rate over the past 200 to 300 years and portends future extinction rates escalating to 10,000 times the background rate. It is understood that out of the nearly 30 million extant species on Earth 32 per cent of amphibians, 23 per cent of mammals, 12 per cent of birds, 25 per cent of conifers, and 52 per cent of cycads are threatened with extinction (*The American Biology Teacher*, vol. 73, no. 2, 2011, p. 80). The human world has not remained unaffected. Irreversible impact has been recorded, on both the physical and psychological well-being of the individual, leading to the growing ethos of 'the survival of the fittest'—socially, psychologically and economically.

The growing field of Humanities has not remained unresponsive to these changes. Much effort has been made to integrate varied fields of study including environmental studies, environmental history, postmodern geography, neurobiology, cognitive rhetoric, multicultural and postcolonial studies for the common goal of ushering in a world that is duly sensitive to the environmental health and the survival of the non-human world. A remarkable effort in this direction is the 'Forum on Literatures of the

Environment', a special issue of *PMLA* 114.5, October 1999 with a call for comments on the growing importance and expanding scope of the fields of environmental literature and ecological literary criticism. Responding to the call Lawrence Buell explained the term 'ecocriticism' as referring to 'literature-and-environment studies', Buell outlined some of the aims and objectives of this field:

1. Consideration of the possibilities of certain forms of scientific enquiry (e.g. ecology and evolutionary biology) and social scientific enquiry (e.g. geography and social ecology) as models of literary reflection;
2. textual, theoretical, and historical analysis of the platial basis of human experience;
3. study of literature as a site of environmental-ethical reflection—for example, as a critique of anthropocentric assumptions;
4. re-theorization of mimesis and referentiality, especially as applied to the representation of the physical environment in literary texts;
5. study of the rhetoric (e.g. its ideological valences of gender, race, politics) of any and all modes of environmental discourse, including creative writing and extending across the academic disciplines and (indeed even more important) beyond them into the public sphere, especially the media, government/corporate organizations, and environmental advocacy groups; and
6. inquiry into the relation of (environmental) writing to life and pedagogical practice. (1999: 1091)

Since the publication of Buell's exhaustive definition, there has been no looking back. The field of ecocriticism has burgeoned with seminars, conferences and individual expressions aimed at promoting the spirit of environmental praxis that has become common at the national and international levels. The history of ecocriticism can be summarily divided into three waves.

As Laurence Buell, Ursula Heise and Karen Thornber note, the first-wave writings of the 1990s, rooted in deep ecology, displayed the tendency of equating the environment with nature, with a focus on literary representations of the natural world in all genres of literature, including non-fiction. These writings looked into the biological, psychological/spiritual bonds between the two entities—human and non-human. The commonalities were explored in the spirit of ecocentric/biocentric ethics and environmental justice for the purpose of ecological conservation. Some noteworthy writers and critics of this period are Henry Thoreau, William Wordsworth, Robert Frost, Thomas Hardy, Wendell Berry and Gary Snyder ('Literature and Environment', www.annualreviews.orghttp://environment.harvard.edu/sites/default/files/Buell HeiseThornber ARER2011 LitandEnvt pdf, environment.harvard.edu.).

The second wave of ecocritical studies gained its strength from the environmental justice movement, taking in its purview the rural, urban, and suburban environments, overcoming the nature-human disjunction to see both as, what Greg Garrard calls, 'interdependent and mutually constitutive' ('Problems and Prospects in Ecocritical Pedagogy', Academia.edu.). This phase too gave prominence to the world of nature. In the late 1990s and early 2000s, the postcolonial approach made its mark with the place-based focus shifting to 'displacements'. The prominent writers/poets relevant to nature writing during this phase were Henry Thoreau, John Muir, Aldo Leopold, Rachel Carson, Barry Lopez, and Annie Dillard. The critical theories considered were Deconstruction, New Criticism, Feminism, Psychoanalytic and Bakhtinian among others. Writers such as Gary Snyder, Adrienne Rich, Willa Cather, and Alice Walker were the stars of this phase. Cheryll Glotfelty (*The Ecocriticism Reader* 1996) traces the third wave of ecocriticism to ecofeminism, questioning the binaries such as nature/culture, mind/body, men/women, etc., and holding them responsible for a disjunction between humanity and nature. Garrard believes that in this phase, the gaze of the critic extended from the rural to the urban landscapes—the 'built environment'.

In the conference held at Trinity College, Dublin in 2011, entitled 'Literature and Environmental Conservation: Responsibilities', I remember agreeing with John Elder's view regarding the need for revisiting the texts written in English before the term 'ecocentricism' became current for the purposes of environmental reading. Some of the older texts included in this volume conform to this spirit of environmental enquiry while some others are new but equally thought-provoking.

New Delhi   SHIVANI JHA

1

The Slackening Tie

Analysing the Changing Bond between Humans and the Environment in Selected Works of T.S. Eliot and Ernest Hemingway

SHIVANI JHA

EARTH'S CHANGING ENVIRONMENT and the increasing vulnerability of its fragile ecological system have been a cause for universal concern for some time now. Ecocriticism has its roots in the expression of this concern. 'Barely, 10,000 years after the end of the Ice Age, the planet is sweltering in some of the highest temperatures in recent earth history.' The scourge of environmental degradation in addition to overpopulation, resource depletion, etc., have led to the heightened vulnerability of modern society to natural calamities, such as earthquakes, tsunamis, floods, and volcanic eruptions—a situation that needs to be taken seriously (McGuire 2002/2014: 2). This predicament has evoked serious note from not just environmentalists and other natural scientists but also writers and thinkers across disciplines, including literature. Ecocriticism has, thus, emerged as a response to the changing dynamics of the relationship between man and mother earth and the need for a more responsible stance on the part of the human world vis-à-vis nature.

In keeping with the aim of ecocriticism of bringing about environmental justice for the non-human world a re-examination of the attitude of a culture towards nature through the study of its literary texts is called for. Cheryll Glotfelty, a renowned ecocritic, defines ecocriticism as 'the study of the relationship between literature and the physical environment' (1996: xviii). Jean Arnold, another eminent critic, describes the paradigm as a 'scholarly site that engenders fertile cross-disciplinary and cross-cultural analysis' (1996: 1089). Jonathan Levin observes the challenges for ecocritics and maintains that they should, (1) convey the impact of a fuller understanding of natural phenomena—especially one drawing on resources associated with natural history, earth sciences, and new scientific fields like complex systems theory, ethology, and cognitive science, thus providing a unique perspective whose emphasis is first and foremost on cultural and social context, (2) stick to the middle ground available to the critic who would understand the dynamic and elusive relation between nature and culture and, (3) bring about a criticism that will do full justice to the natural world and to the social and cultural contexts that shape man's relationship to that world. He finds it imperative that ecocritics face these questions squarely, in order to preserve what has been the most distinctive edge of their work so far (2002: 186).

For an exhaustive discussion of the ideas raised, this essay has been developed on a two-pronged note of: (1) discussing literary works that explore how earlier human beings were living in sync with nature—a way of life that has since been eroded and (2) the impact of that erosion on the human as well as the non-human world, thus establishing the need for empathy towards the environment and the non-humans, so as to buttress the slackening tie between them for a more environmentally sustainable world. To substantiate my arguments, I have used Ernest Hemingway's *The Old Man and the Sea* and selected works of T.S. Eliot, ranging from 'The Hollow Men' to 'The Rock'. The essay is divided into two parts. The first part dwells on the slackening tie between the human and the non-human world. The second discusses the spirit of communality shared between the two, indicating two contrasting ways of existence, one in sync with the natural world and the other existing at its expense.

It has been observed that what people think about themselves in relation to the things around them has an important bearing on what they do about their ecology. In hunting and gathering societies human-environment relations were based on the ethos of reciprocity. Anthropologist Gisli Palsson is of the view that in the spirit of communalism such societies regard the activity of hunting as a relationship 'where hunters and their prey seduce each other', and animals are not viewed as lower entities but as 'social persons'. Such thinking erases the binary of 'nature' and 'society' and sees both as inextricable parts of the universe (196: 74). It is this ethos that finds expression in Hemingway's character Santiago. However, with the transformation from hunting and gathering society to an agrarian one there was a remarkable change in the attitude towards nature. The spirit of communality shared so far was replaced by that of domination, appropriation, and commodification. The permanent forms of agriculture led to new social hierarchies based on wealth, status, and power. Lynn White Jr. notes that human ecology has been deeply conditioned by man's beliefs about his 'nature and (density), i.e. by religion' and blames Judeo-Christianity for technology's devastation of the environment reasoning that it separated heaven from earth. This separation, according to him, established the ideal of a single transcendental god and human domination (1967: 155). A way of life had, thus, definitely ended and a society had come into being which would, with the passage of time, be exceptional for its social and technological progress, bringing about phenomenal comfort and luxury, though not without its perils and pitfalls.

Reading the Slackening Tie between the Human and the Non-human World and its Repercussions as Seen in the Selected Poems of T.S. Eliot

In his path-breaking work *The Third Revolution* (1992), Paul Harrison makes a revealing study of how modern lifestyle and the resultant pollution have impacted the environment and the non-human world in irreversible ways. In the mid-1980s, around 217 billion tons of industrial wastewater was pumped out and it was expected that by the year 2000 the figure would rise to 468 billion tons. Fertilizers and pesticides aggravated the adverse impact on the environment leading to widespread water problems in the form of eutrophication. This affected 30 to 40 per cent of water globally, including 28 out of 65 lakes in Italy, 35 out of 75 in the former West Germany and many of China's lakes. In Latin American countries, 56 per cent of lakes and reservoirs were found affected. In Germany's Black Forest, around the 1960s, drought and disease, along with discolouration, shedding of leaves and needles, thinning of crowns and canopies and decreased resistance to frost were noted.

In the late-1970s, it was also found that a third of the forest's firs were dead, and symptoms of oncoming death had begun to appear on spruce, oak, and birch. Forest deaths, Harrison cautions, are mostly due to human interference affecting the atmosphere. Dumping of acid wastes impacting the quality of soil and acid rain, a result of gases emitted by burning fossil fuels, harm both flora and fauna.[1] He adds, '[I]t is not resource crisis but pollution crisis, and our solid, liquid, and gaseous wastes are the cause of the problem. It is hitting other species first, just as the rise of cyanobacteria massacred the methanogens. But we cannot rely on evolution, or Gaia, to muster compensating forces.' These are prophetic words, '[L]ife may survive in some lowly form. We may not [*sic*]' (1992: 53–4).

Taking into consideration the contingency of ceaseless environmental degradation impacting both the human and the non-human world Jean Arnold opines, 'It is time for all of us together to examine through criticism of written texts our own attitudes towards nature and to engender a sense of accountability for the havoc culture's left hand wreaks on its right hand through shortsighted technological practices' (*PMLA*: 1090). Carolyn Merchant expresses a similar view that science can no longer be considered value-free and proponents of ecocentric ethics should look to ecology for guidelines on how to resolve ethical dilemmas. Merchant particularly emphasizes upon the importance of the harmony of the ecosystem and moral responsibility of humans (1992: 75).

Human interference with the ecological system was bound to boomerang; the non-human world would not suffer alone. Merleau-Ponty's perspective on the subject/object, perceiver/perceived becomes quite pertinent here as shifting the focus from the perceived to the perceiver and his world, he firmly grounds the subject into its context and believes that the perceived ends up revealing the perceiving subject. He says, 'the body will draw to itself the intentional threads which bind it to its surroundings and finally will reveal to us the perceiving subject as the perceived world'. He elaborates upon the often-ignored paradoxical condition of human subjectivity that humans are both a part of the world and coextensive with it, constituting but also constituted (as qtd. by Reynolds http://www.iep.utm.edu/merleau/). As already warned by scientists and other experts, industrialization and urbanization augmented by population growth brought in their wake unprecedented societal changes including perceptional changes regarding the notion of good health and lifestyle, altered engagement of people with the community and the subsequent decline in community life. Unemployment, which was a direct consequence of urbanization, led to a lowered self-esteem, along with changes in consumer behaviour, cultural and religious practices as well as leisure activities (Sahoo, Mishra and Pinta 1985).

Regarding human nature, Karl Marx (1970) posits that the productive life, the free, conscious activity is the 'species-character' of human beings and the object of work is the realization of (human's species') life. Through labour humans are engaged in reproducing themselves intellectually, in consciousness, and through their practical daily activities. However, the working life under the capitalist mode is devoid of this conscious, free, creative activity and characterized by alienation. Analysing this (sense of alienation) in the modern society, Marx hypothesizes that, by essence a creator, the human finds that in concrete, historical contexts his creative urge is crushed resulting in a loss of gargantuan proportions, from that of having a hold over his work processes to exploitation and expropriation and finally of estrangement from all that is human and creative in him.

Taking the analysis a little further, Max Weber (1946) reads rationalization as the root cause for humans' disenchantment with the world, with the growth and intensification of bureaucracy, resulting from the rationalization of the labour-management relationship of government, religion and culture.

He believed that the intellectual ability would ultimately lead to its own nemesis [1946: 363].

Martin Heidegger posited that within the modern technological order, like nature human beings too are liable to become enframed (*gestalt*) as standing reserve. Heidegger's critique of modernity is akin to Adorno and Horkheimer's account of the 'dialectic of enlightenment' whereby the domination of nature is shown to entail both self-alienation through the domination of the body and social domination through economic exploitation and political repression (Rigby 2004: 429). Irish poet Louis MacNeice puts this fear into verse as the cry of an unborn child scared to take birth in such a society, '...O fill me/With strength against those who would freeze my/humanity, would dragoon me into a lethal automaton,/ would make me a cog in a machine, a thing with/one face, a thing' ('Prayer before Birth': http://www.artofeurope.com/macneice/mac1.htm).

In his essay 'Femininity and Masculinity in City-Form: Philosophical Urbanism as a History of Consciousness', Abraham Akkerman vis-à-vis Gilbert Ryle points out Plato's ascetic notion of the Ideal and suggests that habitual urban regimentation of inhabitants is moulding their behaviour as if they were fashioned 'out of waxwork', an eerie prophecy of the impact modern city form would have upon humans resulting in automatism in behavioural patterns (2006: 243).

Sartre's description of a city and its residents in *Nausea* reiterates the notion of the mechanical existence of city dwellers. With contempt he describes city life as, 'trained water running from taps, light which fills bulbs when you turn on the switch, half-breed, bastard trees held up with crutches', with their temperament, 'a little morose' and the successive days of their life, 'simply, a new today' with continued sameness as its characteristic feature (Sartre, as qtd by Akkerman).

It is no surprise then that during the interwar years (World War I and II) when the industrial society witnessed the breakdown of every form of community life, acute self-consciousness and the feeling of death-in-life came to define the postmodern individual. The new world view that came about challenged the spiritual and imaginative life, and humans were caught within their own web of sense impressions. It was believed that behind the sensed phenomena there was no hope for a credible world. Walter Pater wrote in 1868:

Experience, already reduced to a group of impressions, is ringed round for each one of us by that thick wall of personality through which no real voice has ever pierced on its way to us, or from us to that which we can only conjecture to be without. Every one of those impressions is the impression of the individual in his isolation, each mind keeping as a solitary prisoner its own dream of a world. (qtd. by Lester Jr. 1968: 75)

Reflective of these traits, Eliot's characters, the modern men and women, are a defeated lot weary with life and its cares, waiting for rejuvenation.[2] Eliot comments on the work culture when he talks of 'ceaseless labour' or 'ceaseless idleness' or 'irregular labour' for the industrial set up, which had become the lot of the people. There was no regularity in their functioning—it was too much toil followed by (a much needed vacation) or irregularity for want of a constant work opportunity. The kind of work ethic followed in the agricultural set-up was totally lost. In the new scenario the working environment provided no relief for a tired mind and humans functioned mechanically.

J.F.C. Fuller, author of *Atlantis: America and the Future*, warns against the rising level of mechanization in a society boasting of industrialists and manufacturers like Henry Ford, 'In the Ford system, the worker ceases to be a human instrument (in place) he becomes a mechanical tool; craft disappears, and the man is moulded by the machine' (cited in Denton 2001: 6). In such a society virtues like charity, goodness and kindness were all sacrificed at the altar of utilitarianism, and humans focused their attention only on monetary profit. Reflective of these changes Eliot writes in 'The Rock': 'The lot of man is ceaseless labour,/Or ceaseless idleness, which is still harder,/Or irregular labour, which is not pleasant. . . . All men are ready to invest their money/ But most expect dividends/I say to you: Make perfect your will./ I say: take no thought of the harvest,/But only of proper sowing' (46–59).

Eliot's vision of the industrialized society takes into account the mechanical quality of life and the consequent ravages brought upon the human spirit. He finds people having turned indifferent to religion, as religion has failed to satisfy their spiritual needs. The elderly man in 'Gerontion' is the prototype of a generation, which would continue to suffer the feeling of irreparable loss: 'I have lost my sight, smell, hearing, taste and touch / How should I use them for your closer contact?' (59–60).

The chorus from 'The Rock', symbolizing the voice of the Church, profoundly laments this sense of spiritual, religious, and moral bereavement when it asks, 'Where is the Life we have lost in living?/Where is the wisdom we have lost in knowledge?/Where is the knowledge we have lost in information?/The cycles of Heaven in twenty centuries/Bring us farther from GOD and nearer to Dust' (14–18).

Commenting on Eliot's vision, Pericles Lewis points out that, 'Eliot bemoaned the rise of atheism, but also the replacement of the Christian God with new "gods", the abstract intellectual forces like Dialectic and the Earthly values like Money that seemed to have replaced religion for modern age' (2008: 19).

Literary historian Edward Albert delineates this period ranging from 1918 to 1939 as possessing 'an atmosphere of hustle and restlessness never known before'. Ruefully noting the absence of 'calmness of spirit and leisure of mind' during the period, he remarks that both at work and during leisure 'the demand was for more and faster action, stronger and more violent stimulus' (2000: 509). Emblematic of such times Eliot's characters bespeak lack of peace and contentment: 'On Margate Sands/I can connect/Nothing with nothing' (*The Waste Land*, 300–3).

The modern humans, little more than 'hollow men', are perceived as devoid of defining character traits and essence. During the interwar years when the industrial society witnessed the breakdown of every form of community life, acute self-consciousness and self-defeatist thoughts with the feeling of death-in-life came to mark the modern individual. Eliot's 'The Hollow Men' succinctly sums up the prevalent human consciousness when the characters introduce themselves as: 'We are the hollow men/We are the stuffed men/Leaning together/Headpiece filled with straw. Alas!/Our dried voices, when/We whisper together/Are quiet and meaningless As wind in dry grass/Or rats' feet over broken glass/In our dry cellar' (1–10).

In *The Waste Land*, Eliot's London comes across as an 'Unreal City,/ Under the brown fog of a winter dawn,/A crowd flowed over London Bridge, so many, I had not thought death had undone so many/Sighs, short and infrequent, were exhaled And each man fixed his eyes before his feet' (160–5). It is a city of losses. People here are seen as having lost their vigour faring in the journey of life like automatons; the environment is polluted; the winter dawn is shrouded in not clean but 'brown' fog. The sighs and the downcast looks of men with their gaze planted at their feet are symptomatic of their internal misery, and to use Dana Phillip's phrase, 'the erasure of the distinction between life and death' (1996: 209) is complete.

Exploring the Spirit of Communality between the Human and the Non-human World in Hemingway's *The Old Man and the Sea*

History indicates approximately ten million men having been killed during the First World War, from August 1914 to November 1918. This was one of the most tragic incidents in the history of the West and its impact on the psyche of individuals was deep and devastating. But whereas the fallout of this devastation in the characters of Eliot is marked by feelings of futility and despair, for Hemingway's characters endurance would be the code for survival. The celebrated 'Hemingway code' is, thus, a defining trait for all his protagonists, from Jake Barnes in *The Sun Also Rises* to Santiago in *The Old Man and the Sea*.[3]

In the era of machines, particularly mechanical warfare, personal courage took a back seat but not so in the works of Hemingway. In the best of his later works, particularly *The Old Man and the Sea*, human activities in which the individual could take a stance came to hold much importance for him. It is not surprising, therefore, that as a complete negation to the inhuman world of warfare and mechanization, Hemingway turned to the world of simplicity and individuality that proximity with natural elements allowed. In such a world humans were not reduced to 'cogs in a machine'. The tale of the old man, Santiago, thus, becomes more of a song of praise for the sacred nature of the action taken, not in a spirit of aggression but in one of respect and harmony.

Tried and tested by time, Santiago displays the twin characteristics rarely found together; the tenacity of a warrior and unparalleled humility. He is a nature lover who finds beauty and joy in the non-human world and 'loved green turtle and hawks'. His appreciation of the hawks borders on poetry. He feels sorry for the turtles, including the huge ones for despite their size he feels that they have human-like features, an observation not many fishermen would be capable of making. The consumption of the turtle eggs and shark liver oil, a practice not followed by many fishermen, further binds Santiago to the non-human world.

Hemingway reveals great empathy for the non-human world through Santiago. The ability to empathize with the non-humans around him elevates Santiago to a much higher level of humanity than that displayed by the ordinary fishermen. Whereas Santiago treats the sea as feminine and with much respect and tolerance, many other fishermen in contrast are impatient, exploitative and abusive, speaking of it 'as a contestant or a place or even an enemy'. But the old man gave her the respect of a feminine entity, 'something that gave or withheld great favours', and so he thinks, 'if she did wild or wicked things it was because she could not help them. The moon affects her as it does a woman . . .' (2003: 23).

Santiago also found himself in complete union with the sea as he rows along as he considered the sea as 'la mar' which Hemingway informs, 'is what people call her in Spanish when they love her' (2003: 23). Glen A. Love slots Santiago as 'a virtual Pleistocene archetype in his keen biophilial awareness and his store of skills' that he finds 'to be the distilled accumulation of generations of tradition' (2003: 127).

Santiago's respect for his great adversary borders on love as he realizes that the two of them are interlinked, literally and metaphorically, in the struggle for survival. He is also sorry for the fish as it swims along in all its majesty, in royal purple as befits a king. One of them must die in the struggle but if the old man wins he is determined to kill the fish in spite of his admiration for it. He has to, for he makes his living from fishing. Earlier even before he has killed the marlin, Santiago is 'glad we do not have to try to kill the stars' (Hemingway 2003: 63). Love comments, 'Santiago reveals a compassion and a complexity in his repeated questioning of his killing of the marlin that makes him less than a good killer' (2003: 128). For the fish, marlin, Hemingway creates the same aura as he does for Santiago. Like the old man, the fish also takes heroic proportions in its fight against its predator, opposing him tenaciously to the last remains of its strength. Both the marlin and the old man become heroes in their fight for the survival of the fittest. Through Santiago's eyes Hemingway describes the fish:

He saw him first as a dark shadow that took so long to pass under the boat that he could not believe its length. . . . It was higher than a big scythe blade and a very pale-lavender above the dark blue water. It raked back and as the fish swam just below the surface the old man could see the huge bulk and the purple stripes that banded him. His dorsal fin was down and his huge pectorals were spread wide. (2003: 77)

Hemingway shows that by virtue of his trade, Santiago is so much in sync with the natural world that he does not have to wait for the arrival of the morning but can sense its arrival. Talking about the 'terns' which are long-winged aquatic birds allied to the gulls, he pities them, for, these birds, he feels, have a difficult life hunting for food in the ocean. In her book, *A Natural History of the Senses*, Diane Ackerman writes, 'We need to return to feeling the textures of life,' which she proposes should be done by 'allowing ourselves a greater degree of sensory indulgence, of really feeling' (cited in Dana Phillips: 206–7). From the ecocritical point of view, *The Old Man and the Sea* perfectly embodies the biophilic affinity that is the hallmark of ecocriticism, simultaneously arousing in the readers a wave of empathy for non-humans and exemplifying through Santiago the consequences of attempts to overreach their limits.

Notes

1. All the figures noted here are from Paul Harrison, *The Third Revolution*, London: I.B. Tauris & Co., 1992, pp. 1–42.
2. The source of all poems of Eliot quoted in this chapter is Manju Jain's *Selected Poems of T.S. Eliot* and *A Critical Reading of the Selected Poems of T.S. Eliot*, New Delhi: Oxford University Press, 1992.
3. As opposed to Jake Barnes, a war veteran rendered physically impotent by the terror of mechanized warfare, Santiago is a fisherman bearing alone the vagaries of age and isolation that accompanied the death of his only family member, his wife. However, neither Jake nor Santiago, despite their plight, suffer loss of manhood. This is an important characteristic of the 'Hemingway code' in which manhood is more of a spiritual concept than a mere physical one. Because they will their own endurance, pride and courage, Jake and Santiago emerge strong as individuals unlike others who despite an appearance of power do not evoke respect.

References

Akkerman, Abraham, 'Femininity and Masculinity in City-Form: Philosophical Urbanism as a History of Consciousness', *Human Studies*, vol. 29, no. 2, April 2006.

Albert, Edward, *History of English Literature*, Oxford: Oxford University Press, 1979; repr. 2000, <Edward Albert-History-of-English-Literature.pdf-Google Drive,docs.google.com>, accessed on 17 September 2014.

Arnold, Jean, 'Forum on Literatures of Environment', *PMLA*, vol. 114, 1999.

Denton, Peter H., *The ABC of Armageddon: Bertrand Russell on Science, Religion and the Next War, 1919–1938*, Albany: State University of New York Press, 2001.

Frazer, James, *The Golden Bough: A Study of Magic and Religion*, London: Wordsworth Editions Limited, 1993.

Glotfelty, Cheryl and Fromm Harold, eds., *The Ecocriticism Reader: Landmarks in Literary Ecology*, Athens, GA: University of Georgia Press, 1996.

Harrison, Paul, *The Third Revolution*, London: I.B. Tauris & Co., 1992.

Hemingway, Ernest, *The Old Man And The Sea*, New Delhi: Rupa (sixteenth impression), 2003.

Jain, Manju, *T.S. Eliot: Selected Poems and A Critical Reading of the Selected Poems of T.S. Eliot*, Delhi: Oxford University Press, 1992.

Lester (Jr.), John A., *Journey Through Despair 1880–1914: Transformations in British Literary Culture*, Princeton, New Jersey: Princeton University Press, 1968.

Levin, Jonathan, 'Beyond Nature? Recent Work in Ecocriticism', *Contemporary Literature*, vol. 43, no. 1, Spring, 2002.

Lewis, Pericles, 'Religion', in *A Companion to Modernist Literature and Culture*, ed. David Bradshaw and Kevin Maiden, MA: Wiley-Blackwell, 2008.

Love, Glen A., *Practical Criticism: Literature, Biology and the Environment*, Charlottesville and London: University of Virginia Press, 2003.

MacNeice, Louis, 'Prayer Before Birth', *Eighty Five Poems*, Oxford: Oxford University Press, 1959.

McGuire, Bill, *Global Catastrophes: A Very Short Introduction*, Oxford: Oxford University Press, 2002/2014.

Marx, K., 'Preface to a Contribution to the Critique of Political Economy', *Selected Works*, Moscow: Moscow Publishers, 1970, p. 181.

———, *Economic and Philosophic Manuscripts of 1844*, Moscow: Moscow Publishers, 1974.

Merchant, Carolyn, *Radical Ecology: The Search for a Livable World*, New York: Routledge, 1992.

Palsson, Gisli and Dana Phillips, *The Truth of Ecology: Nature, Culture and Literature in America*, Oxford: Oxford University Press, 2003.

———, 'Is Nature Necessary', in *The Ecocriticism Reader*, ed. Cheryll Glotfelty and Fromm Harold, Athens, GA: University of Georgia Press, 1996.

Reynolds, Jack and Maurice Merleau-Ponty, Internet Encyclopedia of Philosophy, <http://www.iep.utm.edu/merleau>, accessed on 11 August 2015.

Rigby, Kate, 'On the (Im)possibility of Ecopoiesis', *New Literary History*, vol. 35, no. 3, *Critical Inquiries, Explorations, and Explanations*, Summer 2004, pp. 427–42.

Weber, Max, 'Science as Vocation', in *Max Weber: Essays in Sociology*, ed. H. Gerth and C.W. Muts, New York: Oxford University Press, 1946, p. 363.

White Jr., Lynn, 'The Historical Roots of our Ecologic Crisis', *Science*, vol. 155, no. 3767, 1967, pp. 1203–7.

Wilkinson, Richard G., *Poverty and Progress*, London: Methuen, 1973.

2

Watershed Aesthetics

Towards an Ecocentric Cultural Sensibility

RAMBHAU M. BADODE

ECOCRITICISM HAS BROUGHT into the purview of literary discourses an understanding of cultural units like literature, cinema, painting and architecture, in terms of their dispersal towards plants and animals, and also human relationship with the physical environment. 'Watershed Aesthetics' is an outcome of this interest in the study of cultural expressions in relation to life, environment and the bioregions they inhabit. The term 'Watershed Aesthetics' was used by Lawrence Buell in his path-breaking theoretical engagement with ecocriticism in *Writing for an Endangered World*. The term has scope beyond the watershed imagery that it encapsulates, and its implications involve readings of cultural texts in the context of human consciousness that acts as a watershed and conversely, of water bodies that shape human consciousness and creativity. It also proposes the possibility of seeing how literary and cultural texts hydrate both the discourse and the human imagination.

Buell observes that it is an interesting enterprise to investigate how rivers and water bodies have become cultural and national icons through literature and films. He points out, for instance, how the Mississippi has been used as a metaphor for national identity by various American writers ranging from Mark Twain to Langston Hughes. Similarly, he indicates how the Ganges, an icon of India's cultural identity, is propagated through Indian literature and films. Buell is also of the opinion that rivers and water bodies are not mere cultural icons that function as visual symbols but also rich storehouses of metaphors, plots and forms. For instance, in Mark Twain's fictional oeuvre, the Mississippi is not just a river. In a novel like *Huckleberry Finn*, the plot originates from the Mississippi as it provides an escape route for both Huck and Jim, two getaways. Further, their subsequent adventures and experiences too are water borne. The Mississippi has its own currents and undercurrents, which shape the novel alongside inherent dangers such as the presence of Cottonmouth[1] and the flash floods. Huck and Jim negotiate these adventures, as they know the river is also, rather paradoxically, their only way to freedom. Further, the Mississippi also shapes the formal principles of the novel. It accounts for the novel's episodic structure, accidents, coincidences, separation, and reunion of Huck and Jim, and the eventual liberation of a black slave. At the metaphorical level, the Mississippi stands for the primordial gush of water and human blood, both of which connote unrestrained movement. The riverine system in the novel with its branches and tributaries also stand for the veins and arteries that carry the basic pulse of life. A close reading of *Huckleberry Finn* along the course that the Mississippi takes in the novel shows that the river too is a stakeholder in the novel, with its own free will, behaviour, and moral considerations. Thus, the Mississippi transforms in Mark Twain's 'environmental imagination' into an interconnected ecosystem itself in which human beings like Huck and Jim, though integral, are relatively insignificant in comparison to the currents of the river. The Mississippi also influences the readers' imagination as it helps them to perceive the human struggle against the unnatural practices of slavery and racism, by contrasting them to the natural flow of water.

Buell also points out that in the context of 'Watershed Aesthetics', there has been a shift from the image of the river to a watershed. A river, he reminds, has an anthropocentric connotation while watershed is more ecocentric. It is often impeded with man-made structures like dams, canals and bunds. Besides, a river is often (personalized) and humanized by poets and writers. Thames, for instance, is feminized in the poetry of Chaucer, Spencer and T.S. Eliot. Such an act of humanizing a river reduces the force of a river, though it helps the poet or writer to describe its properties, and, thus, define it. Watershed, in contrast, is an ecocentric concept that connotes unrestrained force. This image of water bodies is similar to the one held by Native American and aboriginal cultures. It is possible, hence, to classify literary and cultural texts in terms of rivers and watersheds by aligning the water imagery in them to either the anthropocentric rivers or the ecocentric watersheds. It is also possible, as Buell points out, that one can analyse various cultures in terms of the rivers and water bodies that nourish them. Buell explains this primordial, arterial link between water currents and cultures:

Rivers are ancient cultural symbols and rightly so. Without water, no life. Without ample supply, no sizable human settlement. While civilizations have been defined by the arterial rivers without which they could not have come into existence. The Mesopotamian regimes of the 'Fertile Crescent' by the Tigris and the Euphrates,

Egypt by Nile. Indeed, throughout the world, rivers have become cultural icons by dint of size, extent, beauty, imputed sacrality and utility as transportation routes: the Amazon, the Rhine, the Ganges, the Mississippi. (Buell 2001: 243)

Buell observes further that the naturalness of rivers has often been subordinated to their anthropocentric connotations due to their proximity to various civilizations. He also indicates that in European literature, rivers serve as literal waterways to define a rich imperial tapestry. This kind of configuration of a river can be seen in Joseph Conrad's portrayal of Congo in *The Heart of Darkness*, wherein he reduces the river into a stereotypical othering of Western rationality by identifying the Congo with 'darkness'. Hence, Buell prefers watershed as a defining image in understanding the ecocentric, water-based power of nature that permeates in literary and cultural texts. He argues that watershed has the power to become an 'Aesthetic-ethical-political-ecological image' (Buell 2001: 247).

However, Buell resists a textbook definition of watershed and maintains that the notion of watershed should be more inclusive and resonant. He aligns his notion of Watershed Aesthetics with Gary Snyder's view in 'Coming into the Watershed':

The water cycle includes our springs and wells, our Sierra snowpack, our irrigation canals, our carwash and the spring salmon run. It's the spring peeper in the ponds and the acorn woodpecker chattering in a snag. The watershed is beyond the dichotomies of orderly/disorderly, for its forms are free, but somehow inevitable. The life that comes to flourish within it constitutes the first kind of Community. (Snyder 1995: 229–30)

What Snyder configures here is a biotic community wherein human and non-human species peacefully coexist, emphasizing how each activity of life or life form depends on the shared supply of water. Snyder also implies that human beings and all other creatures belong to the earth, rather than vice versa and thereby, interrogates the anthropocentric Judeo-Christian notion of the hierarchy of life.

Allied to the notion of Watershed Aesthetics is the concept of Watershed Consciousness, which as Buell explains, is the understanding of human consciousness, especially, its collective consciousness as a potent reservoir of images and themes. The term also carries the activist implication of green writing by suggesting that riverine, environmental problems have been often discussed in literature. For instance, it is possible to read Henry David Thoreau's *A Week* as a discussion on the negative consequences of dams on the migration of fish and other biotic factors. One can say that one of the points in the agenda of Watershed Aesthetics/Activism is to locate this Watershed Consciousness in literature and other cultural expressions in an attempt to evaluate their ecocentric relevance.

Buell proposes Watershed Aesthetics and Watershed Consciousness as critical practice and an operational tool, respectively, in the study of literature, culture, history and other allied discourses. These approaches and tools are especially useful in the study of new literatures, which engage with the more urgent development-conservation paradox. It would be an interesting task to locate Watershed Consciousness in these writings. For instance, one can re-read Rabindranath Tagore's *Muktadhara* or Kamala Markandaya's *The Coffer Dams* in the light of Watershed Aesthetics. These two works will prove how Tagore and Markandaya's respective world views are ecocentric. Markandaya, for instance, in *The Coffer Dams* brings three perspectives that try to define a river. These perspectives are that of the British engineers, of Indian technocrats and the local natives. In an attempt to build a dam across the river, the human stakeholders, other than the 'native tribal', overlook the environmental disaster that the dam can trigger off. The novel ends with Markandaya upholding the earth-centred environmental position by privileging the native natural wisdom of the 'tribal' and by critiquing the egocentric oversight of the technicians.

It is also possible to extend an enquiry of Watershed commitments in apparently non-ecocentric writings. For instance, Salman Rushdie's fantasy novels, *Haroun and the Sea of Stories* and *Luka and the Fire of Life*, can be read to show how rivers, lakes, and seas figure as active stakeholders in the realm of fantasy too. In both these novels, river and sea are identified as the sources of memory and stories. Thus, Watershed Aesthetics can be used as a critical practice to determine the ecological value of a cultural text.

Indian literary tradition has a legacy of connecting water bodies to literary imagination and cultural texts. Expressions like *Kavyadhara* and *Katha Sagar* were used commonly in Indian poetics, implying the reciprocal sanctification of water bodies and literature. They also suggest how poems and stories influence, nourish, and enliven culture and reciprocally, how literary texts are rich storehouses of metaphors, images, and words that indicate water. River poems even make a subgenre in Indian English poetry. They imply the cultural, spiritual and physical links between human beings and a water-centred creative imagination. 'The River Poem' by Mamta G. Sagar is a noteworthy work that connects poetry, riverine system and feminine principles. The terse poem reads:

A River Poem

Inside the river are
the sky, the cloud, and the sun.
In my hands' bowl is the river.

If I throw up my hands,
the river spills in drops, scattering
sky, cloud, and sun all o'er me.

From my hands' bowl, if I drink
the river, then within me,
the sun, the cloud, and the sky.

Tell me, who is in who?

The title rolls the functions of the river and poetry into one, and the images and lines merge the identity of a woman, river, and the elements of nature into a creative blur. Such poems enrich both literature and environment by deifying, sanctifying, and irrigating both the domains.

Note

1. It is a venomous snake, a species of pit viper, found in the south-eastern United States.

References

Buell, Lawrence, *Writing for an Endangered World*, Cambridge, MA: Harvard University Press, 2001.

Snyder, Garry, 'Coming into the Watershed', in *A Place in Space: Ethics, Aesthetics, and Watersheds*, Washington, DC: Counterpoint, 1995.

3

An Ecologic Overview from Genesis to Apocalypse

Interpreting God, Nature, Human, Animal and Beast in the Bible

BINI B.S.

T HE BIBLE IS A POLYPHONIC and complex text, and it is difficult to read it as giving a singular, monolithic view on what I would call in the rest of the chapter, 'ecologics'. By ecologics, I suggest that the natural and moral environments comprising the divine, the human, other living beings, the natural world of elements and inanimate matter, and the diabolic are depicted with an implicit logic in the Bible. The multilayered and fluid relationship between each component in this ecologically constructed environmental view asks for a nuanced interpretation. My idea of ecologics is fashioned along Timothy Morton's conceptualization of ecology:

Ecology includes all the ways we imagine how we live together. Ecology is profoundly about coexistence. Existence is always coexistence.... Human beings are each others' environment. Thinking ecologically isn't simply about non-human things. Ecology has to do with you and me. (2007: 4)

The Bible, a 'multivalent' text that emphasizes man's right to control and utilize other creations, also upholds love, compassion, and mercy that human beings should have for one another and the rest of the creation. The Old Testament and the New Testament approach these attitudes and virtues in remarkably distinct ways. The possible assemblage of the Bible as a single sacred canonical text by collecting and combining stories and chronicles existent in a space like ancient Israel indicates the inevitable presence of multiple voices. Different kinds of narrative documents and oral traditions were put together in the Bible during its first stages of compilation. The process of compilation of the Bible is also indicative of a politics of inclusion and exclusion. It is a text with several versions and translations. The narrative of the Bible has both descriptive and prescriptive undertones. While dealing with the textuality of the Bible, the caveat by Mikhail Bakhtin is pertinent: 'The represented world, however realistic and truthful, can never be chronotopically identical with the real world it represents, where the author and creator of the literary work is to be found' (1981: 256).

It does not make sense to see the Bible as a monologic text. The vying voices of the interpretive communities in ancient Israel that wove sacred stories and anecdotes into the narrative of the Bible constitute it as a polyphonic text. As Bakhtin rightly observed: 'A poetics cannot, of course, be divorced from social and historical analyses, but neither can it be dissolved in them' (1984: 36). Reading the Bible is entering a plane of dialogic, rather a multi-logic imagination. In this context, one can also think of the *Dead Sea Scrolls*, Gnostic and apocryphal texts, and the Nag Hammadi library.[1] Making sense of the 'spatiality' and 'temporality' of events from 'creation' in the Book of Genesis to 'doom and judgment' in the Book of Revelation by forcibly tracing a chronological and continuous narrative pattern in the Bible is not the method followed in this chapter. Instead, I have gathered some disjointed and fragmented instances relevant to the study.

The Anti-Environmentalist and Pro-Environmentalist Interpretations of the Bible

In the context of a growing environmentalistic ethos, no religious text other than the Bible is critiqued and at the same time used as the promise of a panacea in the West. Critics of the anthropocentrism promoted by the Bible hold the world view presented in the text, responsible for man's ruthless exploitation and domination of earth and its resources. The Bible, according to this stance, is seen as a clandestine cultural force that incited human beings to establish and sustain control over animals, plants and natural resources. Lynn White Jr. opines that 'Man shares, in great measure, God's transcendence of nature. Christianity, in absolute contrast to ancient paganism and Asia's religions (except, perhaps, Zoroastrianism), not only established a dualism of man and nature but also insisted that it is God's will that man exploit nature for his proper ends' (2004: 197).

The Book of Genesis can be read as explicitly sanctioning man's monopoly over the earth. The belief that flora, fauna and inanimate things are endowed with a divine spirit, as professed by certain Graeco-Roman, Oriental pre-Christian and pantheistic traditions, was eventually rejected by the Christian world. This kind of secularization of nature challenged the sacredness previously attached to natural spaces. As a result, the faith in the spirits of natural objects, which protected them from human invasion vanished leading to the indiscriminate exploitation of nature. The practice of placating the living spirit of nature before cutting a tree, building a bridge or killing an animal became forbidden.

The Bible deals with topography in a symbolic way. The rivers, seas, mountains and trees have a metaphoric significance in the biblical landscape. This does not seem to be a resacralization of the earth in conformity with certain pre-Christian traditions. Kate Rigby's reading of the mountains in Graeco-Roman and Christian traditions as the 'touchstone for differing perceptions of the relationship among God, humanity, and nature' (2004: 135) illustrates the various contexts in which mountains and vales figure in the pre-Christian and Christian texts. Mount Olympus is the house of Greek Gods. Mount Ararat is where the ark of Noah landed after the floods. Moses receives the law on Mount Sinai. Many incidents in Christ's life, like overcoming the temptation of Satan, take place on mountains. Jesus does place the high over the low in a hierarchical relationship in his teachings and some theologians tend to transpose this view to topography. However, Isaiah's prophecy that 'Every valley shall be exalted, and every mountain and hill shall be made low' about the scenario after the coming of the Messiah contrasts this hierarchical understanding (qtd. in Rigby 2004: 134).

Christianity, unlike polytheism, pantheism and other religious practices of nature-worship in certain parts of Europe, Asia, and Africa positioned man and nature in an ambivalent and dichotomous relationship. The Old Testament, especially the Book of Genesis is open to an interpretation that sanctions insensitivity to natural objects. It needs to be remembered that people's conception of the environment depends on what they think about themselves in relation to things around them. Religion plays a vital role in constructing an ecological view. In this context, Christianity's condemnation of and triumph over certain pre-Christian, polytheistic and pantheistic traditions should be studied carefully. This triumph is facilitated by colonialism. Lynn White Jr.'s argument is that substituting the sacred divinity of nature with an anthropomorphic God intensified the ecological crisis. White Jr. avers that 'The whole concept of the sacred grove is alien to Christianity and to the ethos of the West. For nearly two millennia Christian missionaries have been chopping down sacred groves, which are idolatrous because they assume spirit in nature' (2004: 199).

The instructions about conservation and non-destructiveness in the Old Testament of the Bible often seem to emanate from a utilitarian outlook. This passage clearly states that:

When you besiege a city for a long time, making war against it in order to take it, you shall not destroy its trees by wielding an axe against them. You may eat from them, but you shall not cut them down. Only the trees that you know are not trees for food you may destroy and cut down, that you may build siege works against the city that makes war with you, until it falls. (Deuteronomy 20: 19–20)[2]

It is sinful, according to the Bible, to worship nature, which is a creation and not the Creator. In pre-Christian and pantheistic traditions, people worship the creation and fertility Gods so that their cattle and crops flourish. The Bible warns against nature worship and assures that accepting monotheism will bring a shower of blessings on the believer. Passages like, 'They exchanged the truth about God for a lie, and worshiped and served created things rather than the Creator—who is forever praised' (Romans 1: 25) and 'The fruit of your womb will be blessed, and the crops of your land and the young of your livestock—the calves of your herds and the lambs of your flocks' (Deuteronomy 28: 4) clearly state what is expected of a true Christian and what he should not be doing. Joseph Campbell argues that:

What the Old Testament, read as history, tells is the very violent story of the conflict between Yahweh and the nature Gods of Canaan. The kings are forever going over to the nature Gods, sacrificing over the hilltops, 'doing what was evil in the sight of the Lord'; and the mighty Goddess, she of many names, who is the true and ultimate deity of nature and of the muses, who brings forth and nourishes all life, and of whom the Gods are the agents, is known there as 'the Abominable'. (1997, 2007: 257–8)

Removal of the sacred feminine who was worshipped as the mother who brings forth and sustains all creations and substituting the notion of divinity with a stern, powerful male God is a very significant episode in the desacralization of nature. In Christianity, the conflicts between the traditions that portray an omnipotent, omnipresent singular God in opposition to the forces of nature and the Graeco-Roman Dionysian strains are evident. Despite all attempts to wipe out the polytheistic and pantheistic traditions, they survived in different guises such as the Virgin and the saints in Christendom.

It is also interesting to note that several movements aimed at the conservation of nature and environmentalism sought inspiration from the Bible, especially the principles of mercy and compassion in the text. For instance, the ecotheology movement that aspires to make philosophy and spirituality companions of social transformation focuses on a reinterpretation of the Bible. The movement takes issue with the view that the Bible validates man's domination, control, and even exploitation of other animate and inanimate beings and resources of the earth. Brian Baxter, an ecotheologist, recommends enlightened anthropocentrism in his Ecologism. A new ideology and set of moral concerns about the earth, which is a home where humans should coexist emerged at the fearful thought of an impending catastrophe.

The attempts towards preserving biodiversity do not always originate from biophilia, but mere survival instincts and utilitarianism. Ecological justice is often founded on the view that human beings are dependent on other forms of life and resources that the green planet houses.

Many Christian environmentalists think of the idea of stewardship as a functional and useful step towards the conservation of earth and its resources. The idea of stewardship is based on the biblical assertion that everything in this universe belongs to the creator and man, the crown of creation is accountable for other creations. There are several biblical verses affirming this idea.[3] Stewardship in Christianity has as its foundational principle that human beings are creations of the same God who created the universe. So it becomes a true Christian's responsibility to look after the earth and he/she should respect this gift given to humanity for its use and delight. The wise and cautious use of the earth and its resources, which is a gift to humanity is at the core of the environmentalist and conservationist agenda of stewardship that involves a strong moral agency. By doing so, human beings become collaborators in the divine work of creation, sustenance, redemption, and sanctification amounting to a kind of protectionism of the environment. Two major examples of stewardship are seen in the Book of Genesis. In Genesis 2: 15, it is stated: 'The Lord God took the man and put him in the Garden of Eden to work it and take care of it.' Another example is the story of Noah and his ark. Humankind's first attempt towards the conservation of nature and other creatures is described in this Biblical story. Noah was commanded by God to preserve life. This story is a source of inspiration to many Christian environmentalists. The destruction of life by flood is a powerful metaphor. When God entrusts the role of the saviour of 'sinless' and 'clean' living beings to Noah during the deluge, the stewardship is affirmed in unequivocal terms. The covenant between God and the living creatures on earth does give an assurance of divine protection, but not an assurance of unconditional forgiveness from the divine.[4] The idea of eco-ethical consumption seeks inspiration from the warning against greed, gluttony, and covetousness in the Bible.

Eager to Please the God: Sacrifices in the Bible

Sacrifice is a ritual practice in several religions. The Vedic tradition of Aswamedha and the sacrificial rites in Graeco-Roman, Semitic and Islamic traditions are performed in order to celebrate victory, thank or please the divine and sometimes to seek forgiveness for sins committed. The biblical God of the Old Testament reminds human beings often about the abundant blessings showered on them and several expressions of gratitude are demanded, sacrifice being one of them. Rene Girard who has studied sacrifice in the Judeo-Christian world extensively says: 'Sacrifice takes place when sacred violence takes charge of the victim; it is the death that produces life just as life produces death, in the uninterrupted circle of eternal recurrence common to all the great theological views that are grafted upon sacrificial practices—those that do not acknowledge the demystifying effect of the Judeo-Christian tradition' (1978, 1987: 226).

Girard evaluates the fundamental difference between Christ's passion and all the other sacrifices that preceded it. The Bible, especially the Old Testament, has several stories of animal and human sacrifice. Rene Girard analyses human sacrifice and the process by which sacrifice becomes ritualized. Substitution of animals for people as it happened in the case of Isaac highlights the cathartic aspect of it. The rituals include not only killing and burning flesh, but sending away an animal into the wilderness before that as evident in the Exodus. The process is described like this: 'Aaron shall lay both his hands upon the head of the live goat, and confess over him all the iniquities of the children of Israel, and all their transgressions in all their sins, putting them upon the head of the goat, and shall send him away by the hand of a fit man into the wilderness.'[5]

It is stated in the Old Testament that the pleasing aroma of burning flesh is dear to God. God, according to the story, favours Abel's animal sacrifice to Cain's offering of grains. The preference to Abel's blood sacrifice is read by Girard as a sign of the sacrificial protection on which all social order will be founded: the mass and massive violence aimed at all will be kept controlled by the ritualized violence of all against one. Cain stands for the chaotic, bloodthirsty mob in the grip of a murderous frenzy whose target is a single victim, a scapegoat. Abraham's son Isaac's sacrifice was demanded by god, and later the child was substituted by a ram. The whole procedure of this ritual atonement is highly symbolic.[6] Girard observes how sacrificial rites are based on mimetic impulse and two fold substitutions:

The first is provided by generative violence, which substitutes a single victim for all the members of the community. The second, the only strictly ritualistic substitution, is that of a victim for the surrogate victim ... it is essential that the victim be drawn from outside the community. The surrogate victim by contrast is a member of the community. (1972, 2005: 284)

Sacrifice, symbolic and real, is depicted as a pious mediation between the human and the divine. Exodus and the first seven chapters of Leviticus have rules regarding animal and food sacrifices. These offerings are supposed to be burnt so that god can enjoy the aroma. Human sacrifice is also mentioned in the Bible. Baptism is symbolic of death through which the sin of the flesh is righted and washed clean. Jephthah burns his only daughter Mizpah to please the Lord after his victory over the Ammonites (Judges 11: 34); King Josiah executed the priests of the shrines of non-believers on their own altars, and burned human bones to desecrate them (2 Kings 23: 20). The call to burn non-believers is emphasized in several episodes of the Old Testament of the Bible.[7]

Jesus privileged mercy over sacrifice. He states: 'Go and learn what this means, "I desire mercy, not sacrifice." For I have come to call not the righteous but sinners' (Matthew 9: 13). Rene Girard has analysed the parallels between the scapegoat and a martyr with respect to the passion of Christ and persecution of saints. The death of Jesus on the cross is understood as a sacrifice and is linked with the offering of the Passover lamb. Jesus is symbolically called the 'lamb' and the good shepherd. So the sacrifice is of the Son of God who is an amalgamation of the divine and the human—the 'good shepherd' who came to take care of humanity. For redeeming their sins, his body is sacrificed, like that of a lamb. The Eucharist, also called the blessed sacrament, reminds of the fact that during the Last Supper, Jesus gave his disciples bread, saying, 'This is my body', and wine, saying, 'This is my blood'. What Jesus says through a violent metaphor in John (6: 53–6) 'Whoever eats my flesh and drinks my blood remains in me, and I in them', is an evocation to partake in the eternal life, which is made possible through his sacrifice to redeem humanity.

God, Man, Animal and Satan: The Ecologic of the Bible

In this section, I have analysed the complex relationship between God, nature, human, animal, Satan and the diabolic beasts and their roles in the biblical universe. Certain incidents in the Bible can be read as sites for interaction between the categories of the 'divine', 'nature', 'the human', and the 'diabolic'. The hegemonic and polyvalent associations among these categories are depicted with an implicit 'hierarchic arrangement', which is deemed essential for maintaining the moral order and a vaguely defined cosmic balance. According to traditional interpretations, in the cosmological arrangement upheld by the Bible, God and the human male (created in God's image) dominate everything else—women, animals, plants, and all other matter are placed at descending levels of subordination. This hierarchical plan suggests roles, functions, and identities to God, human, non-human and the possible relationships that connect and deploy them in the cosmic arrangement implied here. When the word 'god' is used in a biblical context, the difference between Jehovah (Yahweh) of the Old Testament and Jesus Christ of the New Testament has to be kept in mind and also the idea of the Trinity in which the Father, the Son, and the Holy

Spirit are embedded. Though the Bible endorses the idea of One God, it is not fiercely a monolithic and monologic entity.

Certain codes of conduct and ethical norms pertaining to these multilayered interactions and relationships are woven tactically into the biblical narrative to ascertain the need to conform to the divine plan, thus demanding obedience. I argue that the ideas of virtue, reward, sin, and punishment are embedded in the narrative with a particular ecological view. It is not an apolitical symbiotic relationship of categories that the Bible is talking about. In the Bible, the unequivocal definitions of boundaries and limits for man, woman and every living creature, overt warnings about transgressions and their consequences, and above all, the reiteration of the unchallenged supremacy of divine authority are not accidental.

My argument is that the Bible recommends a particular, though somewhat loosely defined perspective on God, man, woman, nature, and devil in actual and metaphoric ways. It is evident in the history of Christianity and the Church that those vested with power and spiritual authority had on several occasions strictly dealt with violations of norms. One of the Bible's very prominent assertions is that God is the sole creator and the one who has the power to sustain and destroy the universe. He has authority over the heavens and the earth. Through the words of the Old Testament prophets, especially Isaiah and Moses, God often reminds that He is their Creator. There are several passages in the Bible that highlight the greatness of the Creator.[8] One has to remember that in a polyphonic text like the Bible, to arrive at a single theory about God's equation with his creations is difficult. The elements of authoritarianism and compassion are mixed in the persona of the biblical God and these diffused shades of his character influence his dealings with nature, man and other animate beings and inanimate objects.

In the Bible God's role does not end with creation; He sustains and exercises control over his creation.[9] The Bible also represents nature and the forces of nature as under God's control, which he uses many a time to carry out his purposes and realize his plans.[10] The complex polyvalent narrative of the Bible enters into the discursive, dialogic fabric of human life and into the world symposium in a Bakhtinian sense. The heteroglossic character of the biblical narrative makes it practically impossible to define the hierarchical relationship between God, man and nature into a single pattern. One cannot unambiguously and indubitably state that Christianity asserts the superiority of man over all other creations, because the ideas of love, compassion and mercy are equally prominent in the text. However, its anthropocentrism is most evident in the Book of Genesis. The Book of Genesis is used by traditional interpreters of the Bible to assert that the creator considered man a unique creature, superior to other creations. Woman was derived from man, created from his rib because God found man sad in his loneliness, craving for a companion. Genesis (1: 26, 1: 28) asserts man's superiority over other living organisms and earth.

Adam was given the right to give names to all the animals, thus asserting his authority over them. What man sought in the animal world was a symbol in the Christian context. Robert Fossier draws our attention to the complex animal symbolism in certain biblical anecdotes: 'The donkey that the Lord chose as his mount was the symbol of holy humility; the dove with the olive branch in its beak was the sign of lessening divine wrath; the fish, the Greek name for which (ichthys), was the symbol of Christ, the fisher of souls' (2007: 191). The Book of Genesis gives the impression that God designed all of the earth for man. Every other creation was intended to serve man's purposes. The body of Adam was made of clay, but that does not make man a mere component of earth. Northrop Frye's remark that, 'We know only of a world in which every human and animal form is born from a female body; but Bible insists, not only on the association of God with the male sex, but that at the beginning the roles of male and female were reversed in human life, the first woman having been made out of the body of the first man' (1981, 1982, 1983: 107) is indicative of how the Bible validates the patriarchal ethos and rejects the prevalent 'mother earth' concept. Though Adam is created by a male God from dust, no sacredness is assigned to the material that went into the creation.

Christianity sees humans as divided into flesh and spirit, and its condemnation of the flesh and the world as inferior to the realm of the soul is often explicit. The philosophical approaches, affirmative of the body, were overshadowed by theories denigrating and condemning it. Sanctity of the body is emphasized by equating it to the temple of God.[11] This view is contrasted by the statement, 'the desires of the flesh are against the Spirit, and the desires of the Spirit are against the flesh' (Paul, Galatians 5: 1).

The Book of Genesis is used by traditional theologians to portray the earth as corrupt and degenerate because of the 'original sin'. The Hebrew for man (adam) sounds like, and may be related to the Hebrew for ground (adamah) and so is the name Adam.[12] Ecotheologists believe that the spirit-dust concept calls for a new understanding of the divine, since it implies the multiplicity of spirit and its physical and elemental links to the soil and earth.

Though nature worship and pantheism were rejected as ungodly ways of life, the early Church understood nature as a symbolic system through which God communicates with the crown of his creation, man. In the Old Testament, God uses elements like fire and water, natural forces like avalanche and storms and creatures like locusts to punish the sinners and destroy them and their property. The flood in Noah's time, the fire that destroyed Sodom and Gomorrah, attack by locusts on Egypt, famine and drought created by God on several occasions, the shower of manna and quails from the sky are but some biblical instances that exemplify how nature participates in God's plans to reward and punish. In this artistic rather than scientific outlook, like in a fable, elements of nature, plants, and animals have moral lessons to teach man. Though the Bible does not attach any intrinsic value and sacredness to earth, there are warnings about the defilement of land and consequent punishments. Earth is depicted as created for man by God. Man's 'sins' and 'misdeeds' contaminate it and often divine wrath comes in the form of a destructive catastrophe. Lust, greed, disobedience of the commandments, 'unnatural behaviour' such as homoeroticism, sex with animals, sluggishness, blasphemy, lack of faith, worship of other Gods, and the like, are deemed to contaminate the land, which invites divine ire. There are plenty of examples on the reciprocity of defilement of land and punishments from God that befall as famine, epidemics and other disasters.[13] Ecclesiastes 3: 1–8 states that there is 'a time to plant and a time to uproot, a time to kill and a time to heal, a time to tear down and a time to build, a time to keep and a time to throw away' implying the preordained disposition of nature's mechanisms. Abuse and exploitation of the resources, waste, greed, and haste are deemed wrong and begetting punishment. Man is told that 'You are the salt of the earth' (Matthew 5:5) which not only means a main ingredient, but something that prevents the decomposition of flesh, the symbol of temporal life. Consider this passage from the Old Testament: 'The earth lies polluted under its inhabitants; for they have transgressed laws, violated the statutes, broken the everlasting covenant. Therefore a curse devours the earth; its inhabitants suffer for their guilt' (Isaiah 24: 4–6).

The proverbs in the Bible often use nature to instruct man. The example of an ant is cited as a warning against sluggishness in Proverbs 6: 6–11 and Proverbs 30: 24–8. Many of Christ's parables and teachings took examples from nature to instruct his disciples. These parables could directly and effectively communicate to a people whose occupations were closely associated with nature. Parables of the mustard seed, vine, barren fig tree, labourers in the vineyard, good shepherd, wheat and weeds, lost sheep, seeds secretly growing, one who sows and reaps, and the like, use instances from the familiar world and occupational practices of the agricultural and pastoral community whom Jesus addressed. The Apostles also followed the same pattern of selecting known examples from the natural environment. Matthew 6:26 affirms: 'Look at the birds of the air; they do not sow or reap or store away in barns, and yet your heavenly Father feeds them. Are you not much more valuable than they?'

Similar passages found in both the Old Testament and the New Testament[14] serve the purpose of asserting the fact that nature is a strong channel through which the divine revelation percolates to the human realm.

Nature teaches about God and also through nature God's wisdom and holiness are revealed to human beings. The dependence of man on God is intensified due to the fact that the very natural forces that man needs for his survival in an agricultural and pastoral set-up were portrayed as under the control of God.[15]

Leviticus states several laws regarding eating animals of land, sea, and air. A hierarchy is established among animals, birds, and fish by dividing them as clean and unclean or kosher and non-kosher. The idea of man's physical sanctity is implicit in this warning against eating unclean meat. Disposal of dead animals, both clean and unclean and norms of purification of the human body after that also validate how the Old Testament emphasizes the purity of the human body. But in the New Testament, these rules are not presented as inviolable mandates. Paul affirms that humans have the liberty to eat whatever they wish: 'For every creature of God is good and nothing is to be refused if it is received with thanksgiving; for it is sanctified by the word of God and prayer' (1 Timothy 4:1, 3–5).[16]

The Book of Genesis also implies that there are limits to man's authority and his knowledge. The idea of sin is based on disobedience in the Book of Genesis. Sin and salvation are woven into the biblical narrative as a grand plan designed by God. The condemnation of woman as the 'Door of the Devil' by St. Bernard is founded on Eve's temptation by the serpent. The tree of knowledge of good and evil, the fruit of which was forbidden (Genesis 2: 16–17) was also created by God. Man's domination was curbed by God's punishment for the sin of disobedience and the resultant expulsion from the Garden of Eden.

The biblical God does not want to allow man to claim equality with or superiority over his creator and master. The expulsion from the Garden of Eden is not only an aftermath of disobedience, but also reveals God's concern that the human being, who has started understanding what is good and evil by eating the fruit of knowledge, might dare to eat the fruit of the tree of eternal life and become immortal. God states: 'The man has now become like one of us, knowing good and evil. He must not be allowed to reach out his hand and take also from the tree of life and eat, and live forever' (Genesis 3: 22). The right to immortality is granted only to those who remain obedient to the end. Revelation 2:7 reads: 'He, who has an ear, let him hear what the Spirit says to the churches. To him who overcomes, I will give the right to eat from the tree of life, which is in the paradise of God.'

The Bible firmly states that though man is created in God's image, it does not entail him to be like God. The story of the Tower of Babel is an example of how God suppresses man's desire to touch the sky of glory.[17] The Bible seems to suggest that the 'Fall of man' unleashed chaos in the relation between God and man, between man and woman, and between all human beings and nature. Humans then were subjected to the laws of necessity and had to learn and master survival tactics, which altered their world and world view. The end of toil free existence marked the beginning of man's struggle and even fight with natural forces for survival and sustenance. With the sin and the Fall of man, the whole creation was corrupted and still awaits the day of deliverance (Romans 8: 18–25). The salvation which God promised man also includes the redemption of the rest of His creation (Colossians 1: 19–20). The redemption is always futuristic, which coincides with a moment of the resolution of all conflicts. The Bible portrays a harmonious, conflict free relationship between the different creatures of the earth.[18] Isaiah (11: 1–9) illustrates a dream of the coextensive spirit:

The wolf will live with the lamb, the leopard will lie down with the goat, the calf and the lion together, and a little child will lead them. The cow will feed with the bear, their young will lie down together; and the lion will eat straw like the ox. The infant will play over the cobra's den, and the young child will put its hand into the viper's nest. They will neither harm nor destroy on all my holy mountain; for the earth will be filled with the knowledge of the Lord as the waters cover the sea.

A beautiful picture of life in harmony with nature is also given in the description of the Garden of Eden before the Fall. The prophet imagines the reign of God and the resultant peace, security, and tranquility on the earth. The recurrence of similar motifs can be found in the portrayal of the Promised Land and the garden in the 'Song of Songs' ('Song of Solomon'). 'The Song of Songs' depicts the sensual and sexual encounters of the man and woman, which are conspicuously absent in the Book of Genesis and other books of the Bible. The inscription of the natural world in the human body is found in the 'Song of Songs'. The enjoyment of the woman's juices as 'honey' and 'milk' is reminiscent of the descriptions of the Promised Land as 'flowing with milk and honey' (Exodus 3: 8, 17; 13: 5; 33: 3). Earth is attributed feminine characteristics in these passages. The flora and fauna in 'Song of Songs' act as a backdrop and a channel of ecstasy in the process of actual, sexual creation in contrast to the asexual one in the Book of Genesis. The sexual union of Adam and Eve is portrayed as an aftermath of their sin. On the other hand, we perceive an exultation and exaltation in the union of the man and the woman in the 'Song of Songs'. Season of spring is also implicated in the verse. The comparisons of man and woman to flowers and animals indicate how the song sees nature as deeply connected to the human world. The woman is described as the garden and its flowers (2: 1 and 4: 12-5: 1), and the man as an apple tree (2:2) and as henna blossoms (1:14). Animals also enter this scheme of things. The man is compared to a deer, a gazelle and a stag. Humanity and nature are entwined in the 'Song of Songs', and it is remarkable that human beings are depicted as seeking ecstasy in nature and the relationship is sensuous and not didactic or moralistic.

Besides the categories of God, human and nature, angels and devils are part of the ecologics of the Bible. In the hierarchy, angels are above human beings, messengers of God who assist him. The fallen angels form the category of devils. Satan, symbolic of evil, also known as the Devil, Diablo, Beelzebub, the Beast, the Dragon, the Serpent, the Prince of the nether world and the like, is seen as the adversary of God, and once a favourite creation, the luminous one or Lucifer who rebelled against the divine authority. He tempted Eve and tried to tempt Christ in the wilderness. The King James Version of the Bible commonly uses the term 'devils', whereas some other translations use 'heathen Gods,' 'idols', etc. There is an argument that the Gods worshipped in pre-Christian, pantheistic traditions are being condemned as evil in the Bible. Exorcism symbolically may refer to the expulsion of pre-Christian deities. Descriptions of Satan and demons may be attempts to explain frightening and destructive natural occurrences that were beyond the grasp of a pre-scientific consciousness. The iconography of Satan and other demons combine elements from animal bodies, such as hoofs and horns. The depiction of evil in the Bible can be interpreted as a way of warning against the animalistic, unbridled, and instinctual elements of the human spirit.

The two beasts described in Revelation are also depicted as diabolic manifestations. The First Beast who arises out of the sea has seven heads and ten horns. The Second (Lamb-like) Beast arises out of the earth and speaks like a dragon. This Beast exercises authority on behalf of the First Beast, causing humans to make an image of the First Beast and worship him.

The Bible does prophesy the end of the world and this eschatological strain is most evident in the Book of Revelations. It is a polyphonic apocalyptic document though there are short apocalyptic passages in the Gospels and the Epistles. In this Book we can see a conglomeration of the realms of heaven, earth and hell occupying their respective places and playing roles in the confrontational drama of the forces of good and evil. The Lamb, the Dragon, the archangel Michael and a number of other angels, the Beast from the Land, the Beast from the Sea, the great harlot Babylon, the four beasts around the throne of God, the four horsemen of the Apocalypse, the two witnesses, the woman clothed with the sun, and the narrator (John) are part of this cryptic narrative. Timothy Morton observes that 'Christian apocalypticism shares with deep ecology a fundamental lack of concern for the way the things are going. Since the end of the world is nigh, or since we will all become extinct in the long run, there isn't much point in caring' (2007: 27).

The triumph of the Lamb, symbolic of Christ's victory over the antagonist, Satan, who appears as the dragon is a major thematic interest of the apocalyptic narrative, which prophesies regeneration after the destruction.

Ultimately, the dragon, the Beast. and the False Prophet are thrown into a lake of fire. The four horsemen who ride white, red, black, and pale-green horses symbolize conquest, war, famine, and death (or pestilence), respectively, and their appearances coincide with the opening of the seals by Jesus. The Book of Revelations also gives the assurance that God's people will inherit a New Earth, which is closely associated with the prophecies in other books of the Bible.[19] In some theological environmental movements, this idea is used in an interesting way, hinting that the present environmental crisis is based on a biblical prophecy, and hence inevitable; also there is hope for the godly who will prevail on a regenerated earth.

Ecotheology and Christian Environmentalism

The Biblical God is described as the Creator who, as Creation unfolded, 'Saw everything that He had made and found it to be very good.' A critic of orthodox Christianity, Lynn White Jr. observes that 'we shall continue to have a worsening ecologic crisis until we reject the Christian axiom that nature has no reason for existence save to serve man' (2004: 191). On the other hand, in the twentieth and twenty-first centuries, many movements for the conservation of nature emerged, seeking inspiration from the teachings of the Bible. Pope John Paul II is quoted as saying: 'The ecological crisis is a moral issue'...'the responsibility of everyone', and that the 'care for the environment is not an option'.[20] The Pope recommends an ecological conversion. The Catholic Church often projects the ecological crisis as a religious crisis. The views expressed in 'A Pastoral Letter on the Christian Ecological Imperative' also testify the same:

While beginning to listen to the experiences of the marginalized in society, we must also be attentive to the cry of the creation that surrounds and sustains them. Whereas we once began by developing critical analysis of economic, political and social structures that cause human suffering, we must now also bring the additional riches of ecological justice to bear on such realities.[21]

However, most of the popular concerns for the conservation of the earth are ultimately pragmatic and utilitarian, i.e. nature has some material worth in the discourse and practice of a utilitarian framework. Nature's diversity and fecundity are seen only as commodities, as natural resources have entered the capitalist paradigm as things that can be bought and sold, exploited, used, and abused at one's whim.

In contrast, deep ecology professes an environmental philosophy that expresses 'the idea that nature has intrinsic value, namely, value apart from its usefulness to human beings, and that all life forms should be allowed to flourish and fulfill their evolutionary destinies' (Taylor and Zimmerman 2005: 456). A similar spirit is found in the philosophy of St. Francis of Assisi. In his 'Canticle of the Sun', St. Francis addressed the sun and the moon as beings who shared with him the bliss of being alive: 'My Brother the Sun, my Sister the Moon, our Mother the Earth, my Brother the Wind, our Sister Water, and Brother Fir' are not mere rhetorical devices but kinship terms indicative of deep-rooted nature mysticism. Glimpses of a similar spirit can be found in Henry David Thoreau, William Blake, William Wordsworth and writers of the Romantic period. Nature mysticism celebrates the joy, serenity, and deep philosophy of nature. It is also an insight into the dependence and interrelatedness of all elements and beings of nature. This view has aesthetic, scientific, and idealist nuances in it.

Rachel Carson is an environmentalist who distances herself from the biblical paradigm and argues that all lives are interrelated in deep spiritual ways. Viewed in this light, the right to control nature and the conviction that nature exists for man are baseless assertions of the human ego. Ecological humanism implies an awareness of humanity as part of the natural world. Everything on earth, its flora and fauna, is part of a web of life comprising multilayered relations between all components. Even while disturbing these relationships out of sheer necessity, the awareness that we would have to suffer the consequences is required. Timothy Morton takes a stance critiquing the obsession with deep ecological ethics based on a spiritual and metaphysical philosophy. According to him, any movement based on the philosophy of 'healing the nature to compensate the damage done' is bound to give unrealistic expectations about human activities and lifestyles and may even lead to technophobia. In Morton's opinion, nature that has a spirit shining through it is an idealistic myth. This view may sound as the assertion of another mode of anthropocentrism, which is more inclusive and pragmatic.

I presented these new ecological views in juxtaposition to selected biblical interpretations to show the ways in which they conform to and differ from the Bible. My intention in the essay is not to read the Bible as the main cause for the current ecological crisis. Neither am I trying to prove that it has several inspirational subtle messages that have the potential to offer handy solutions. The 'ecologics' of the Bible that has a bewildering array of books, testaments and gospels, is multifaceted and intricate; it cannot be comprehended using any monolithic logic. The depiction of hegemonies, hierarchies and relationships in the Bible is so nuanced that it is hard to locate any fixed places assigned for God, devil, man, and nature in its scheme of things. This essay is an attempt to approach the text, respecting its polyvalence, trying to decipher and interpret its polyphonic voices and place it in the context(s) of topical ecological and environmental debates. I do not claim this reading to be conclusive or exhaustive.

Notes

1. In December 1945, near the town of Nag Hammadi in Upper Egypt, an Arab peasant found thirteen papyrus codices containing fifty-two sacred texts, which are representatives of the long lost Gnostic Gospels. The discovery of the Nag Hammadi texts has fundamentally revised our understanding of both Gnosticism and the early Christian church.
2. Quotations from the Bible are from the New International Version.
3. See the 'Introduction', pp. 7, 1–12.
4. Psalm 24: 1, Deuteronomy 10: 14, Leviticus 25: 23 and Job 41: 11 affirm the superiority of human beings over all other creatures.
5. See Genesis 9: 8, 10, 12–13, 16–17 to read about the nature of the covenant.
6. Leviticus 16: 21. This and the following verses give detailed instructions for the procedure.
7. See Leviticus 21–26 to understand the rich symbolism of sacrificial rites.
8. See Deuteronomy 13: 13–19, which directly commands to punish the non-believers.
9. See Psalms 24: 1–2, 33: 6–9, and 89: 11, Colossians 1: 16 and Revelation 4: 11, which unequivocally assert the supremacy of God.
10. See Psalms 65: 9–13, 147: 7–9, 12–18 and Jeremiah 10: 13 to understand the nature of God's control of man and the universe.
11. See Psalm 104: 21–30 and Job 37: 2–13 for several instances in which God carries out his will through nature.
12. See 1 Corinthians 3.16–17, 1 Corinthians 6.19 that use the metaphor of the temple to describe the human body.
13. <http://www.biblegateway.com/passage/?search=Genesis+2%3A7&version=NIV>, accessed on 9 May 2012.
14. Warnings about 'Defiling the Land' can be found in Jeremiah 2: 7, 12: 4, and 12: 11; Ezekiel 34: 17–18, Hosea 4: 1–3 and Romans 8: 22. Consequences of Defiling the Land are described in Psalm 107: 33–4, Isaiah 5: 8–10, Jeremiah 3: 2–3 and Revelation 11: 18.
15. See Psalm 147: 9, Job 12: 7, 10, Psalm 19: 16 in which metaphors of nature are used to illustrate ideas.
16. Old Testament passages Deuteronomy 11: 8–17 contain explicit warnings and the promise of abundance.
17. See Genesis 11: 1–9 to read the story of the Tower of Babel.
18. See Isaiah 11: 6 and Ezekiel 34: 25.
19. 'I saw a new heaven and a new earth; for the first heaven and the first earth had passed away, and the sea was no more' (Revelation 21: 1). See also Isaiah 65: 17, 66: 22 and 2 Peter 3: 13.
20. Pope John Paul II, Peace with God the Creator, Peace with all of Creation (World Day for Peace Message), 1 January 1990, no. 10.
21. 'A Pastoral Letter on the Christian Ecological Imperative', from the Social Affairs Commission, Canadian Conference of Catholic Bishops, 4 October

2003 on the Feast of St. Francis of Assisi, Patron Saint for Ecology. The text is available on <http://www.cccb.ca/site/Files/pastoralenvironment.html>, accessed in July 2015.

References

Bakhtin, Mikhail, *The Dialogic Imagination: Four Essays*, ed. Michael Holquist, tr. Caryl Emerson and Michael Holquist, University of Texas Press Slavic Series, no. 1, Austin: University of Texas Press, 1981.

———, *Problems of Dostoevsky's Poetics*, tr. Caryl Emerson, ed. Godzich and Jochen Schulte-Sasse, *Theory and History of Literature*, vol. 8, Minneapolis, Minn.: University of Minnesota Press, 1984.

Bax, E. Belfort, *The Decay of Pagan Thought*, 1890, S. Sonnenschein & Co. in, <http://www.marxists.org/archive/bax/1890/01/pagan.htm>.

Baxter, Brian, *Ecologism*, Edinburgh: Edinburgh University Press, 1999.

Buell, Lawrence, *The Environmental Imagination: Thoreau, Nature Writing and the Formation of American Culture*, 1996.

———, *The Future of Environmental Criticism: Environmental Crisis in Literary Imagination*, Malden: Blackwell Publishing, 2005.

Campbell, Joseph, *The Inner Reaches of the Outer Space: Metaphor as Myth and as Religion*, California: Joseph Campbell Foundation, 1986, 2002.

———, *The Mythic Dimension: Selected Essays (1959–1987)*, California: Joseph Campbell Foundation, 1997; 2007.

———, *Flight of the Wild Gander: Explorations in the Mythological Dimension, Selected Essays (1944–1968)*, California: Joseph Campbell Foundation, 1951, 2002.

Carson, Rachel, *Silent Spring*, Mariner Books, 1962; 2002.

Deane-Drummond and E. Celia, *The Ethics of Nature*, Malden: Blackwell Publishing, 2004.

Elder, F., *Crisis in Eden: A Religious Study of Man and Environment*, Nashville, TN: Abingdon, 1970.

Fossier, Robert, *The Axe and the Oath: Ordinary Life in the Middle Ages*, tr. Lydia G. Cochrane, Princeton: Princeton University Press, 2007.

Frye, Northrop, *The Great Code: Bible and Literature*, New York: Harvest Book, Harcourt, INC, 1981; 1982; 1983.

Girard, Rene, *Violence and the Sacred*, tr. Patrick Gregory, London: Continuum, 1972; 2005.

———, *The Scapegoat*, tr. Yvonne Freccero, Baltimore: The Johns Hopkins University Press, 1986; 1989.

———, *Things Hidden Since the Foundation of the World: Research Undertaken in Collaboration with Jean Michel Oughourlian and Guy Lefort*, tr. Stephen Bann and Michael Metteer, California: Stanford University Press, 1978; 1987.

Glotfelty, Cheryll and Harold Fromm, eds., *The Ecocriticism Reader: Landmarks in Literary Ecology*, Athens: The University of Georgia Press, 1995.

Hall, D.J., *Imaging God: Dominion as Stewardship*, Grand Rapids: Wm. B. Eerdmans, 1986.

————, *The Steward: A Biblical Symbol Come of Age*, rev. edn., Grand Rapids: Wm. B. Eerdmans, 1990.

Lewis, Tanya and Emily Potter, eds., *Ethical Consumption: A Critical Introduction*, New York: Routledge, 2011.

Moltmann, J., *God in Creation: A New Theology of Creation and the Spirit of God*, San Francisco: Harper and Row, 1985.

Morton, Timothy, *Ecology without Nature: Rethinking Environmental Aesthetic*, Cambridge: Harvard University Press, 2007.

————, *The Ecological Thought*, Cambridge: Harvard University Press, 2010.

Odum, E.P., *Fundamentals of Ecology*, 3rd edn., Philadelphia: W.B. Saunders, 1971.

Osborn, L., *Stewards of Creation: Environmentalism in the Light of Biblical Teaching*, Oxford, England: Latinex House, 1990.

Reznick, David N., *The Origin then and Now: An Interpretative Guide to the Origin of Species*, Princeton: Princeton University Press, 2010.

Rigby, Kate, *Topographies of the Sacred: The Poetics of Place in European Romanticism*, Charlottesville: University of Virginia Press, 2004.

Taylor, Bron and Michael Zimmerman, 'Deep Ecology', in *Encyclopedia of Religion and Nature,* ed. Bron R. Taylor, London: Continuum, 2005.

Wade, Nicholas, *Before the Dawn: Recovering the Lost History of Our Ancestors*, New York: Penguin, 2006.

————, *The Faith Instinct: How Religion Evolved and How it Endures*, New York: Penguin, 2007.

White, L. Jr., 'The Historical Roots of our Ecologic Crisis', in *This Sacred Earth: Religion, Nature, Environment*, ed. Roger S. Gottlieb, New York: Routledge, 1967; 2004.

4

The Ecologically Lonely and Bereft World of T.S. Eliot's *The Waste Land*

NEENU KUMAR

ECOCRITICISM OR GREEN STUDIES might be loosely defined as an attempt to find new ways of 'studying the concrete conditions of life, space, and *habitus*' (Conley 1997: 2) as they are represented by fictional and non–fictional texts. It has variously been defined as the 'study of the mutually constructing relationship between culture and environment' (Bennett and Teague 1999: 3) or, more specifically, as the 'study of the relationship between literature and the physical environment' (Glotfelty and Fromm 1996: xvii). Lawrence Buell's *The Environmental Imagination* was one of the first major attempts to suggest a preliminary approach to ecocritical interpretations of literary texts. Buell suggests that environmental perception has been neglected by literary history and that ecocriticism endeavours to retrace 'the place of nature in the history of Western thought' (1995: 1). In the essay 'The Ecocritical Insurgency', Buell observes that:

although the term was coined twenty years ago,[1] although critical readings of literary texts ... in relation to ideas of nature, wilderness ... and spatial environments of all sorts have been pursued for the better part of a century, only in the last decade has the study of literature in relation to environment begun ... to assume the look of a major critical insurgency. (1999: 699)

In other words, Buell stresses that even though human ideas about nature and landscape have played an important role in literature the new ecological understanding of the human relation to the non–human environment has encouraged a growing number of scholars to redefine their approach to literary representations of these issues.

Richard Kerridge and Neil Sammells assert the importance of the new ecological viewpoint by stating that 'the starting-point for the ecocritic is that there really is an unprecedented global environmental crisis and that this crisis poses some of the great political and cultural questions of our time' (1998: 5). Both ecologists and modern critics condemn Western civilization's negative impact on human and non-human forms of life. They explain that earth's ecological catastrophe is often understood as 'punishment for human transgression; the necessary consequence of going too far' (1998: 4). They further add that 'the real, material ecological crisis, then, is also a cultural crisis, a crisis of representation. The inability of political cultures to address environmentalism is in part a failure of narrative' (1998: 4). Buell's working hypothesis is based on the premise that the modern environmental crisis necessitates more than a simple redefinition of man's relation to nature. According to him, the current ecological problems should bring about the awareness that this 'environmental crisis involves a crisis of the imagination, the amelioration of which depends on finding better ways of imagining nature and humanity's relation to it' (1995: 2).

Modern industrial societies have exploited and polluted the earth to such a degree that the physical reality of this world has been altered. Therefore, the patterns of human perception need to be adapted to the changing environments. Terry Gifford explains the growing ecological consciousness within literary criticism as: 'Ecocriticism may be the frame of our age, informed with a new kind of concern for "environment", rather than "countryside" or "landscape" or the "bucolic" but we cannot pretend that there have not been changes in our knowledge, attitudes and ideology' (1999: 5).

Ecocriticism, in other words, addresses traditional accounts of the human relation to the non-human world from a new point of view. Indeed, as Roy Willis has observed, 'since the mid-1970s, the academic debate about humanity's relation with the natural world has been profoundly influenced by what is generally called ecology' (1990: 6). From the growing evidence that modern technology and industrial growth has allowed human beings to radically change the environment, the fear arises that our modern industrial societies risk disrupting the basic premise of interrelatedness. Ecocritic Robert Harrison Pogue often stresses that 'ecology names far more than the science that studies ecosystems; it names the universal human manner of being in the world'. Hence, he claims that 'we dwell not in nature but in the relation to nature' (1992: 201). Modern society's problematic conceptions of nature have sanctioned the exploitation of the physical world.

Ecocriticism analyses the shortcomings of past and present conceptions of nature, while at the same time it endeavours to rediscover alternative apprehensions of nature that are part of our cultural tradition. From an ecocritical point of view, it is important to stress that the 'nature-culture distinction is both a distorting and a necessary lens' (Buell 2001: 5) that determines our understanding of the non-human world. Environmental awareness, in its modernist transfigurations, is of paramount importance for issues concerning alienation and authenticity. In his famous essay, 'Postmodernism', Ihab Hassan talks about 'Dehumanization' and also focuses on the 'Denaturalization of the Planet and the End of Man' (1984: 53).

Hassan alludes to the increasing pessimism that lurks behind the incorporation of urban environments into modern literature. He goes so far as to maintain that the majority of urban literature uses the city as an embodiment of disaster (1981: 108). Regarded as an emblem of environmental degradation, the city may be used to delineate the problematic human interaction with habitat and environment. One of the critics most centrally identified with urban literature, Raymond Williams, has described the influential role of the city in modern fiction as a historically embedded phenomenon in which 'the modern wasteland, and through it a powerful convention of urban imagery, became almost commonplace' (1973: 239). In applying this insight to fictional accounts of 'the ugliness and meanness of industrialism and urbanism', he argues that the city in literature symbolizes 'the cancerous results of an outgrown but still rigid and stupid system' (1985: 230). In short, Williams' line of reasoning associates urban imagery with a critique of a modern form of life, which at a time of urban and industrial transformation started to gain impetus. Accordingly, Williams explains the modernist fascination for the city as: 'Struggle, indifference, loss of purpose, loss of meaning . . . have found, in the city, a habitation and a name. For the city is not only, in this vision, a form of modern life; it is the physical embodiment of a decisive modern consciousness' (1985: 239).

Burton Pike points out that the city in literature perfectly mirrors 'man's contradictory feelings—pride, love, anxiety and hatred—toward the civilization he has created and the culture to which he belongs' (1981: 26). It is under the impact of Oswald Spengler that modern authors began to use the city as a metaphor for the degradation of Western civilization. Spengler's theory of the city as a 'Megalopolis' was expounded by Edward Hundert, who points out that the term was used to 'designate the new pattern of our urban life wherein the "city is a world, is the world"' (1968: 107). Spengler's ideas reveal that underlying this preoccupation with metropolitan existence is the insight that this form of human habitat illustrates Western civilization's growing distance from the non-human world. As Ihab Hassan admits, 'the city' has always been a "crime against nature"' (1981: 107). Just as Hassan draws attention to the problematic relation between the city and nature, so ecocritics have theorized that the city reflects modern society's desire to dominate the physical world. Marian Scholtmeijer's analysis of urban imagery, for example, argues for a concept of the city in literature as a symbolical realm, which reflects Western civilization's increasingly conflictual relation with the physical world. Scholtmeijer, therefore, reminds us that underlying the extraordinary variety of urban settings in modern fiction, there is a desire to use the city as an 'expression of antipathy to the civilizing process' (1993: 143). Invoking the city to express a critique of enculturation suggests that the city is a crime against non-human and human nature. Hence, Scholtmeijer reminds us that cities have been 'erected in opposition to nature' (1993: 144). An immediate implication is that the city in literature may be used to express a fear that 'humans are alienated from the natural world by virtue of their enculturation' (Phillips 2003: vii). Scholtmeijer argues that 'the cities we have built to shut out the world seem not to free but to oppress us' and that, as a consequence, 'identity scrambles to find a foothold in the city' (1993: 143). Her ecocritical analysis of urban contexts suggests that it is man's negation of nature, which creates this sense of alienation because it denies that human beings, as natural organisms, are dependent on the physical world as a healthy and meaningful habitat. Cities, thus, exemplify the self-destructive impact of Western culture's domination of nature. Especially the modern metropolis then, reflects how 'the ultimate in human domination of nature ... escapes human control and puts to exile vital aspects of the psyche' (Scholtmeijer 1993: 145).

As pointed out by Lawrence Buell, the 'rhetoric of apocalypticism implies that the fate of the world hinges on the arousal of the imagination to a sense of crisis' (1995: 285). Buell, who stresses the literary tradition of apocalypticism, sees *The Waste Land* as largely focused on such a sense of crisis. He has even gone so far as to maintain that T.S. Eliot has written 'one of the first canonical works of modern Anglo-American literature to envision a dying society' (1995: 288). This sense of apocalypticism is heightened by the city, which in turn breeds alienation.[2] There is a desperation underlying the modern human experience as also a particularly pessimistic undertone of powerlessness and incoherence, which is generated by alienation. Notions of an established order with nature being the provider have been undermined and human beings themselves have become the plunderers of the very nature they were to preserve. This can be seen through the lives of T.S. Eliot's characters, who bear overtones of anxiety and there is a concrete relation between the notion of crisis and a socio-historical sense of alienation. There is a sense of anguish about their own culture which verges on self-destruction. This collapse of a reassuring order results in a high degree of pessimism that is extremely destabilizing. The discord with the harmonious old order gives birth to the grotesque and the monstrous, a world which is full of chaos. Eliot places his readers at the heart of this crisis and depicts a dismal picture of the modern world as a menacing totality. He voices what Miller exclaims: 'we're all dead, or dying, or about to die' (1993: 46). The anxiety 'is in the blood now—misfortune, ennui, grief, suicide. The atmosphere is saturated with disaster, frustration, futility' (Miller 1993: 19–20). The diseased world is an 'empire of neurosis' (Miller 1980: 89), which has further alienated humans from their natural environment.

In the words of Marianne Thormählen, 'A work of art such as *The Waste Land* cannot be subjugated under any one fixed interpretative scheme, it lives its own life in its readers ...' (1984: 40). Looking at it through the lens of ecocriticism is merely touching one aspect of this great poem. Eliot's *The Waste Land* presents a sociological report about people (Madam Sosostris and the young carbuncular, Lil and Albert and the typist, home at tea time), who suffer from and with each other. In it we find 'a gallery of grotesque or desperate figures ... who move on the edges of the city' (Hassan 1967: 60). Through these desperate, grotesque protagonists and alienated figures, Eliot presents their sexual, artistic, philosophical, and existential confrontations with the modern metropolis and its other inhabitants. These inert denizens, who feel unable to come to terms with the excessive patterns of modern life, exemplify the senselessness of metropolitan existence. The threatening aspects of such urban representations express a sense of fragmentation and violence, which insinuates that the narrator experiences his modern habitat as a menacing burden. The theme of the poem encompasses simultaneously several levels of experience arising out of various wastelands: the wasteland of religion in which there are rocks but no water; the wasteland of the spirit from which all moral and spiritual springs have evaporated; and the wasteland of the instinct for fertility where sex has become merely a mechanical means of animal satisfaction rather than a potent, life-giving source of regeneration.

Nature is polluted by many a modern society's dirt. The very water that had been a means of purification (the holy water of Father Thames),[3] immortalized in Shakespeare's *The Tempest* as, 'those are the pearls that were his eyes',[4] is now 'the river [that] sweats/Oil and tar' (ll. 266–7). [Here this is a direct reference to the numerous oil spills endangering aquatic life and, thus, unbalancing the delicate balance of nature]. The physical pollution mirrors the moral pollution of the daughters of the Thames— young girls are being physically used and their 'indifference' points towards an all time moral low. Not only is nature being raped but so is morality.

> Exploring hands encounter no defence;
>
> His vanity requires no response,
> And makes a welcome of indifference. (ll. 240–2)

Christ, who rose after crucifixion, is now being killed by the wastelanders due to their neglect, with the effect that they are living a death-in-life.[5]

He who was living is now dead
We who were living are now dying. (ll. 328–9)

The faith in materialism seems to have conquered over the faith in God, not vaguely but clearly because there was a proposal for the demolition of the church, viz., 'Magnus Martyr' for the building of a hotel.

Of Magnus Martyr hold
Inexplicable splendour of Ionian white and gold. (ll. 264–5)

And, the subsequent:

London Bridge is falling down falling down falling down. (l.426)

Thus, the poem encapsulates what can be termed as living death symptomizing the modern wastelanders.

The commodification and the commercialization of life has turned humans away from nature where there is only 'dead land' (l.2) and 'the dead tree gives no shelter, the cricket no relief' (l. 23). The sea is 'desolate' (l. 42) and 'the mountain mouth [is] of carious teeth' (l. 339). There is only the 'one eyed monster' (l. 52) who is devouring everything in its wake. For most of the denizens of 'the wasteland', there is only the sense of frustration and futility. Eliot emphatically points out that humans are themselves responsible for the deplorable condition of nature. If they coexist with nature, they can contribute to its fertility but their indifference has led to its desolation. Nature, therefore, is no longer able to facilitate growth and rebirth. Instead, there is sterility and death.

What are the roots that clutch, what branches grow
Out of this stony rubbish? (ll.19–20)

In this image, 'roots' no longer sustain but seize flowers as if taking them to a sort of underworld. Nature becomes an uninhabited place by actively denying people's needs, as sterility and exposure replace sustenance and protection. Eliot's description is of a nature that has become malevolent as a direct result of human apathy towards it. The waste within has resulted in the waste outside. The opening lines of the text reinforce this notion of the hostile interaction between individuals and their environment. However, Eliot's malevolent nature does give the possibility for protection and compels the reader to 'Come in under the shadow of this red rock' (l.26) as 'In the mountains, there you feel free' (l.17) but the very next instant it can only offer 'fear in a handful of dust' (l. 30).

The cultural wasteland, that London has become, is uncaring and unemotional towards its inhabitants.

That corpse you planted last year in your garden,
Has it begun to sprout? Will it bloom this year? (ll. 71–2)

In addition to walking the streets, corpses can/will replace flowers in a garden and threaten to overrun beauty with death. Therefore, death overwhelms nature and the sense of desolation becomes more profound because of the incongruous split between the individual and the environment. Eliot records this disintegrating experience of life through the use of powerful imagery: 'A heap of broken images, where the sun beats,' (l. 22); 'The river's tent is broken,' (l. 173), '... I was neither/Living nor dead ...' (ll. 39–40) and so on.

Henry Miller in his novel, *The Air-Conditioned Nightmare*, wonders, 'what have we to offer the world beside the superabundant loot which we recklessly plunder from the earth under the maniacal delusion that this insane activity represents progress and enlightenment' (1945: 20). Eliot's *The Waste Land* also expresses the same angst,[6] which attests to the popularity of the theme of death in life and the anxiety of the modern humans in the face of their relation to the changing environment. D.H. Lawrence calls the modern humans, 'as ghastly simulacrum of life' (1986: 21–49) and, thus, they experience modernity as a malady. The malaise of modern life is that humans are plundering nature and there are 'Cracks ... and bursts in the violet air' (l. 372), clearly referring to the air raids of the First World War. Such environmental concerns seem to emanate from the fact that the issue is that human beings are no longer turning to nature for reprieve. There is a shift of paradigms which has radically altered the modern human's attitude to the physical world. Nature has been reduced to being used and abused without being replenished. The utilitarian approach to the non-human world borders on indifference and callousness. The religious, moral, and cultural degeneration has resulted in human domination of the non-human world on the premise that people have the right to exploit and consume natural resources.

Hassan argues that Eliot has tried to grasp 'the flux of human experience and respond to its random compulsions' (1967: 30). That nature is portrayed not merely as a metaphor for simplicity in an age characterized by oppressive structures of socialization but also, as a victim, clearly comes through lines such as 'the dead tree gives no shelter, the cricket no relief' (l. 23). The human body is also shown as a victim of modernity.

I think we are in rats' alley
Where the dead men lost their bones. (ll.115–16)

Eliot's *The Waste Land* seems to be attuned to the widespread effects of modern civilization, in its industrial, urban, and technological manifestations, on human and non-human organisms. Eliot's characters 'exhibit all the century's feverish desire for . . . meaning when significant human meaning is exactly what they suspect their world and universe may lack' (Nichols 1995: 104). The characters' sense of alienation is certainly accentuated by the theme of death in life. Modernity ushers in a problematic rupture with the past. The modern conception of nature reduces the physical environment to merely a source of energy, in which 'everything is ordered to stand by, to be immediately at hand' (Heidegger 1977: 17). As a result, modern society claims nature as its 'standing-reserve' (Heidegger 1977: 17) without replenishing it. Society's utilitarian conception of nature has contributed to patterns of exploitation, which have enabled the oppression of nature and human beings alike. According to Max Horkheimer and Theodor Adorno, 'what man want[s] to learn from nature is how to use it in order wholly to dominate it and other men' (1979: 4). Consequently, both human beings and the physical world they inhabit, suffer from the exploitative framework of modern progress. Eliot gives voice to the individual's embodied experience of human and non-human environments. The interrelation between the individual's rational mind and a knowable universe is in question. The despair of the modern era and its devitalized life are exemplified by a number of recurrent motifs of anxiety in Eliot's work such as 'dead', 'dying', 'dry', 'broken' and 'red' as the colour of violence and death. The ecological despair about the negative effects of modern progress can be seen through images like 'the dull canal' (l. 189), 'Here is no water but only rock' (l. 331). These are repulsive images, which mix vulgarity and cheap modern decadence. Through these images Eliot has mirrored what Leo Bersani calls the 'mournful sense of the break [of his times]' (1990: 48).

Eliot's depiction of the malaise of modern life in *The Waste Land* leaves a very strong impact on the reader. He uses powerful urban imagery to underline the drama of modern society and present humans' problematic struggle with their environment. Eliot's *The Waste Land* mirrors not only the collapse of harmonious old orders but also the wretchedness and sordidness of the city of London. The gloomy and noisy life of London is like 'Jug Jug' to 'dirty ears' (l. 103). The metropolis becomes an active superorganism, a Moloch that risks destroying its inhabitants. Eliot employs urban imagery to put across a more complex image of the narrator's desperate experience of modern life. Thus, it is the capacity of urban imagery to highlight the narrator's embroilment with modernity that heightens the reader's awareness of the reasons why it is perceived as a malady.

From an ecocritical point of view the question, therefore, arises whether Eliot's depiction of urban environments with images from pathology, points to the belief that modernity has ushered in an environmental crisis. Eliot presents the readers with a city of fragments and meaningless excess.

Whereas the meaninglessness is attributed to the distancing from nature; the fragmented picture of the modern city reflects the problematic experience of a disintegrating urban life. By specifying that this urban habitat is 'dead' and 'barren', the author emphasizes that the malaise of urban life is the direct outcome of Western civilization's unbridled exploitation of nature. From this perspective, the city's struggle with nature parallels the individual's struggle with his or her habitat. The lacerated environment becomes an outward manifestation of the inner collapse. The urban dwellers' profound sense of alienation, the Western civilization's problematic relation with the natural world, and the growing distance between nature and humans are portrayed through profound and recurrent urban imagery.

Interestingly, Eliot called his poem *The Waste Land* and not 'The Barrenland'. There is a difference between the two. Barrenness is a reflection on the quality of land; a 'wasteland' is one whose potential has been wasted by its users. By this subtle choice of epithet to describe today's moral degradation, Eliot shifts the focus from the land to those who have turned it into

> A heap of broken images, where the sun beats,
> And the dead tree gives no shelter . . .
> And the dry stone no sound of water . . . (ll. 22–4)

The utter sense of waste, hopelessness and futility is captured in 'I see crowds of people walking round in a ring' (l. 56). The fault lies with the society that has chosen to grow 'dead people'. In Eliot's 'wasteland', nerves no longer give strength and confidence, the brain no longer thinks, the mind cannot remember and the wind does not produce any effect. It is a land of desolation where every relationship is 'vulgar and cheap'. Eliot's *The Waste Land* is very relevant to contemporary times since environmental degeneration has become far more widespread now than in 1922 when he wrote it. Humans in the twentieth and twenty-first centuries have made garbage a part of their lives by plundering the non-human world and living in the 'waste' of an,

> Unreal City,
> Under the brown fog of a winter dawn (ll. 60–1)

Resources—physical, mental, moral, earthly, heavenly, of whatever nature—give strength, happiness, joy, and fulfilment. *The Waste Land*, on the contrary, is the story of a land where resources of all types are wasted. And the rot has spread across religious, moral, social, and physical aspects of life. It is a continuum of destruction and desolation. The progression of decay has been from religion to morality to social relationship to finally humans' relationship with themselves and with their physical environment.

Towards the end of his poem, Eliot advocates a return to classical Nature to overcome suffering which has come about due to the increasing alienation from nature. The end of Eliot's literary project is instigated by 'visionary impulses'. The remarkable fact about his 'visionary' sense of an ending, therefore, is that 'it prepares for rebirth' (Hassan 1967: 6). Considering the fact that the collapse of orders, which characterizes the crisis of modernity, puts the body in the unique position of active witness and victim of the self-disintegrating spectacle of modern progress, it is obvious that the healing of the human organism is of paramount importance.

> DA
> *Datta*: what have we given? (ll. 400–1)
> . . .
> DA
> *Dayadhvam*: . . . (ll. 409–10)
> . . .
> DA
> *Damyata*: . . . (ll. 417–18)[7]

Interpreted from an ecological point of view, Eliot asks 'what have we given [to nature]?' Eliot appeals to the reader to restrain from plundering, to give back to nature more than has been taken and to be more tolerant towards it. What is significant is that he gives the readers hope for a better future. Eliot ends his poem with the words: 'Shantih shantih shantih' (l. 433). It is a formal ending to an *Upanishad* and can be loosely translated as 'The Peace which passeth understanding'. Eliot seems to propose that human beings can be at peace only if they begin to live in conjunction with nature. 'Peace' and 'understanding' can come if nature is given its due. Raymond Williams in *The Country and the City* discusses the reciprocal relation between urban and rural life. He draws attention to utopian patterns: 'The apparent resting places, the successive Old Englands to which we are confidently referred but which then start to move and recede . . . all these, in fact, mean different things at different times, and quite different values are being brought to question' (1985: 12). This purports the traditional idea that 'man was happiest in the beginning—in the golden age—and that the record of human activity is a record of decline' (Marx 1967: 55). Eliot does not particularly adhere to this idea but what is important to note is the intended message that man has to show reciprocity towards nature if he wants to live a life without anxiety and does not want to remain alienated from it in an urban setting.

The symbolic aridity and decadence of modern Western civilization as well as the poet's own inner despair at the desolate prospect of the post-First World War era, with its chaos and frustration, are aptly presented through *The Waste Land*. Steeped in a melancholic humour, *The Waste Land* unfolds as cold and dry as a rock in the desert night. It focuses sharply on the numbness and utter sterility of modern civilization. Eliot felt that the world was on the verge of total collapse, due to its spiritual, intellectual, and psychological exhaustion. Today's world is also inhabited by dead people and this deadness adds up to the sum total of the desolate wasteland scenario. This wasteland is projected in different ways—as a physical, natural desert as well as a socio-cultural, intellectual, and moral barrenness. Echoes of Eliot's *The Waste Land* find strong resonance in the twenty-first century, and at an amplified scale too.

Eliot's poem addresses not only the emptiness that he perceived around him but also the spiritual 'drought' in his own life. It is a poem begun and rooted within the deep recesses of past memory and it relies upon these connections to make sense of the present and move tenuously forward. His decaying society finds an echo and holds a mirror to the modern world. Thrown into a world of materialism and human isolation, devoid of passion and hope, every human being is seeking, a shower of hope in the midst of the drought to wash the world anew. It is in this sense that Eliot's characters foreshadow the inhabitants of today's world as well.

The Waste Land does not merely put forward an analysis of the prevailing malaise but also offers measures aimed at its correction. (It is the effort of creation that will help humans make sense of the result.) Like the knights roving for the Holy Grail, all human beings will search for a water source to refresh the world even if no such rebirth exists. *The Waste Land* can be read as every human's own quest, varying as it does with the changes of time and tide over a span of years (Gordon 1974: 557). The 'wasteland' can then be conquered only by first understanding it, identifying it, naming it as such and gaining power over it. (The entirety of *The Waste Land* is in the connections that attempt to make sense of some aspects of human experience.) Thus, the poem should be viewed not as a single solid aesthetic 'artifact' but as an exploration of the 'mode of discovery or disclosure' (Spanos 1979: 231) not only for Eliot and his contemporaries but also for the people of the twenty-first century.

The Waste Land attempts to encapsulate a portrait of the past in the image of the future. It is populated with a great number of voices though in the end they may all coalesce into one prophetic sound (Easthope 1983: 332). It is the use of this power of speech which can help conjure names and truths that will bring light to a morally, religiously, and psychologically-dried-up land. Eliot's masterpiece is a creation that will make an inscrutable society into something comprehensible, making sense of the chaotic senselessness (with the ciphers of the past). The poem is not proposing a remedy to the problem of contemporary culture; it is itself the cure. It is less an answer than an exploration of the means by which to attempt to find such answers (Miller 1977: 160–5). Eliot's quintessentially modern 'Unreal City' is any city of the modern world, which was created with little hope of saving the very fragile ecological balance. In this ecologically imbalanced world, human beings are soulless, unbalanced, robotic machines. When the clock strikes the end of the workday, their bodies mechanically turn away from their workstations. Eliot likens their lives to automatons, calling them 'human engine[s] / Like a taxi throbbing[,] waiting' (ll. 216–17). These mechanical humans were as much part of Eliot's times as they are of contemporary times.

Eliot pairs St. Augustine's fervent wish for salvation from worldly lusts to the words of the Buddha's 'Fire Sermon'. The 'Burning burning burning burning' line from the Buddha's sermon, interwoven within Augustine's words, demonstrates Eliot's purpose in unifying East and West to condemn the impotent fires of lust that have spawned the wasteland (308). Both St. Augustine and the Buddha wished for freedom from the body's slavish attachment to sexual passions. The image is necessarily complex, with the element of fire representing both the concupiscent passion and the desire to burn it away (Tamplin 1967: 368). A different, cleansing flame must defeat the selfish fire.

Paradoxically, fire which destroys the good also purges the evil; and hence, in its destruction it purifies. The purification by fire is a turning point in *The Waste Land*, and there is a strange sense of relief in the devastation brought about by the flames. With nothing left to lose, perhaps the world can be reborn from the ashes of its unquenchable fires. The world of lust, selfishness and ennui needs to be cleansed. The topicality of Eliot's poem is such that it provides a solution for the parched wasteland of modern times. Rain comes to the dried and the wasted land giving hope of reviving fertility.

The wasteland and the wastelanders have been given a power of renewal but humanity must choose to embrace it in order for life to be restored. The soul has been given a power beyond reason and Eliot sets up the solution to escaping the wasteland: one must abandon the vestiges of ruined logics, economics and base elements and embrace an understanding of wisdom beyond one's own experience. Of course, death still controls the land but somehow death seems less like an end here than as the beginning of a new life to follow.

In Part V we turn from the setting sun of the west and look to a new sun rising in the east, returning to one of the cradles of human civilization: India. Seemingly from all around, a loud voice booms out,

> Ganga was sunken, and the limp leaves
> Waited for rain, while the black clouds
> Gathered far distant, over Himavant. (ll. 395–7)

The Ganges (or 'Ganga') created a region in northern India of incredible fertility, spawning a civilization and has long been revered by Hindus. Likewise, the Himavat (or 'Himavant') is the Hindu snow-god, the personification of the Himalayas. The speaker's first words frame a connection between the forest, the mountain and the stream that humans would do well to notice. Between the snow run-off and the flooding river basin, the two deities of the mountain and the river normally bring life to a region. Drawing from the ancient Indian text, *The Rig Veda*, Jessie Weston notes the importance of Indian rivers in shaping a culture and suggests how easily the physical river might have become a deity of sorts for the people relying upon its predictable flowing (1993: 25–7, 36, 45). Thus to see the Ganga 'sunken' and a naked Himavant adorned with few white and 'black clouds' is to see the wilderness stretching to all corners of the earth. The wasteland dries up humans like the many 'limp leaves'. Meanwhile the rainless clouds tease them from a far horizon (l. 395). Eliot and also the citizens of the modern world have planted their souls deep in the ground and stomped all over them, wondering why they existed at all.

To the waiting ears, the cosmos utters just a single syllable to the dry lands: 'DA' (l. 400). The reference is to the *Brihadaranyaka*, a section of the philosophically introspective Upanishads. Gods, demons, and humans—each asks the Creator for a message and the Creator responds with the same message for each of them, the single syllable 'DA'. However, each group hears the 'DA' differently, as though it meant the beginning of a Sanskrit word: *Datta* (give), *Dayadhvam* (sympathize), or *Damyata* (control). The parable is concerned as much with how we interpret what we hear, as it is with what the Creator actually intended to say. Eliot uses this as a framework within which to explore the progressions we have made through the wasteland. His words are as true of modern society as they were of his own time.

The gods received the word 'DA' as *Damyata*, to control oneself; humans took the word to mean *Datta*, to give of oneself; and the demons believed the thunder spoke *Dayadhvam*, to sympathize with others. But Eliot rearranges this, suggesting that the order has more significance for his readers if rearranged in this way (Ward 1973: 135–6). Eliot begins with the human interpretation of 'DA' as '*Datta*: what have we given?' (l. 401) 'DA' echoes in the consciousness of the poem's speaker as *Datta*, demanding that modern humans lose their self-centredness and give selflessly to others. This signals a sort of existentialism suggesting that the only escape from ennui is action; one can only escape the aimless boredom of a decadent existence by acting rightly and unselfishly toward one's fellow humans (Brooker and Bentley 1990: 190–1). Lord Krishna says in *The Bhagvad Gita*: 'Your right is only to perform your duty, but never to its results (fruits). Let not the results be your motive, nor you be indolent. Lesson: Perform your duty with a mind free from the anxieties of fruits of action. Neither you be indolent nor consider yourself as the cause (agent) of results' (*The Bhagvad Gita*, Ch. 2: Verse 47).[8]

There is something revitalizing in this sacrifice of oneself (Sorum 2005: 33). It is by these acts—a person reaching out to another, giving (*Datta*) to another, sacrificing one's own safety for the life of another—that we can now live. 'By this', such selfless acts as these, 'and this only, we have existed' cries the narrator (l. 405). Both hopefulness and an admonition are implied here. By saying that selfless giving is the 'only' way humans have ever existed, Eliot is effectively rejecting the selfish world in which he dwells. The Western emphasis on the single individual, isolated from the rest of humanity, is a false paradigm and will only extend to a culture of despair. Life is found in the 'surrender' of every 'moment', in the giving up of power and not in the grasping at strength. To live selflessly in the twenty-first century is not a means of gaining fame and glory—it 'is not to be found in our obituaries'—but it is good and right (l. 406). To act correctly when called upon will 'cover over a multitude of sins' (I Peter IV.8; also James V.20). Eliot invokes the words of ancient Hinduism to combat Western notions of egotism, and with them he demands that humans give of themselves for others to find meaning and hope in life. Here is that strain of existentialism, again, that demands action in order to escape meaninglessness, rather than watching things fall apart from a point of stasis. Without this, there is no humanity, only human lemmings hastening to self-destruction.

Human existence is not to be found in the cobwebbed corners of homes or possessions, nor are lives capable of being stuffed into envelopes, with 'seals broken by the lean solicitor / In our empty rooms' (ll. 408–9). What good is done to fellow humans will far outweigh the broken 'seals' of wills at death; they mean much more than the 'empty rooms' and possessions left behind. The benevolence practised on fellow humans may not come up in wills or 'obituaries', but this is of little importance in the long run. Eliot is here making an argument for orthodoxy. Individual material gains are of little worth compared to the little acts of kindness done to others as they outlive the doer and make for a better legacy for humanity than funeral notices, cobwebbed tombstones, or vast estates. In the first part of the thunder's speech, human beings (particularly Western society) have been instructed with a new ethos: replace the ego-obsessed individual with a consciousness of others. Interestingly, this is an ethic ascribed to by Hindus, Buddhists and Christians alike (among others). (There is always a generic notion of *The Bible* being blamed for colonization and other maladies of Western society, including environmental destruction.) Irrespective of individual gains one amasses in a lifetime, all of one's possessions are utterly empty of value at life's end. It is better to have empty rooms in one's home than in one's soul, since, 'What good is it for a man to gain the whole world, yet forfeit his soul?' (Mark VIII. 36). Likewise, the Buddhist *Udanavarga* says, 'Verily, it is the law of humanity that though one accumulates hundreds of thousands of worldly goods, one still succumbs to the spell of death' (Borg 1997: 71). One must, it seems, lose the self to gain all the rest.

The thunder rolls again, shouting 'DA' into the world consciousness once again, though this time it seems to groan out, '*Dayadhvam*, "sympathize"' (l. 411). Echoes of Eliot's own cries for relief from what he calls the imprisonment that modern life has been reduced to, appear in these lines (Litz 1973: 14). In his 'Notes' Eliot talks about F.H. Bradley's *Appearance and Reality*, a work of philosophy he was much interested in. This 'key' section alludes to Bradley's text, wherein the philosopher suggests that one's experience within the world is as personal and subjective to one's points of view as are one's thoughts and feelings (Bradley 1893: 346). Bradley therein describes what he sees as an error in believing humans can truly understand each other. He writes:

Our inner worlds, I may be told [by one who believes that experiences in the real world are universal], are divided from each other, but the outer world of experience is common to all; and it is by standing on this basis that we are able to communicate. Such a statement would be incorrect. My external sensations are no less private to myself than are my thoughts or my feelings. (1893: 346)

His point is simple: human beings are trapped within their own experiences of reality, unable to look objectively past their own egos to find a means of escaping their confining, solipsistic worlds.

The act of 'Thinking of the key ... confirms a prison' for each person, writes Eliot (l. 414). Even becoming obsessed with escaping our mind-prisons becomes a means of being enslaved to them. 'Only at nightfall', continues Eliot's speaker, 'aethereal rumours / Revive for a moment a broken Coriolanus' (ll. 415–6). In his usual roundabout way, Eliot imagines that humans—the prisoners of their isolated minds—are only able to 'revive' themselves a bit and become aware of their confined situation when everything else has been stripped away (in the darkness and loneliness of the 'night'). Eliot calls these strings of realization within the soul the 'aethereal rumours' of the night winds. This is fitting, as 'What the Thunder Said' is tied to elemental aether from the stars. Symbolically, it requires something outside of the human mind to make people recognize their faults.

Ironically, this 'key' that locked up humanity also contains the power to set its soul free, to escape from the blighted wasteland. Having given of themselves (*Datta*) and given up their power to be selfish, human beings have begun to sympathize (*Dayadhvam*) with their fellow mortals. This sympathy is more than simply renouncing their excess or taking pity on a pathetic figure. To truly sympathize is to become a compassionate person, seeking to understand the suffering of others and help alleviate it. One must first identify with another in order to feel sympathy. A person must not be an isolated giver doing good to a receiver, but must instead realize that the two, the I-ego and the you-other, are not at all different. This sense of compassion comes across in *Mahayana* Buddhist literature. One goal of *Mahayana* Buddhism is cultivating the *bodhisattva*—the mind of a Buddha that takes pity on another and desires to help save the other from suffering (Armstrong 2001: 130). The thunder speaks out against selfishness here, desiring the destruction of the ego preventing us from identifying with our fellow mortals.

The Waste Land is unarguably an account of humanity's failings, the inability to develop the compassion and sympathy needed to prevent a human wasteland. Just as a key was needed to unlock the prison doors, humanity requires element from beyond humanity to set people free again. Thus the aether of the heavens came down to set them free, sending Christ in human form to snap humanity out of its solipsism. It would take an infinitely greater individual to break the bonds of moral, emotional, and social drought. As such, the 'nightfall' that came with Christ's crucifixion (Mark XV.33) ironically brought with it a revival of the human spirit. Following the lead of Christ whose compassion and sympathy made him sacrifice his own life to resurrect humanity from the wasteland, humans themselves can see the escape for humanity. *Dayadhvam* demands that humans do not simply give or give up petty possessions and ideas but that they go further, cultivating a spirit of sympathy for their fellow beings as a protection against the all-pervasive, self-destructive solipsism. It is the only key that will free humans from their self-made prisons.

Thunder rumbles out once more in line 417 as another loud 'DA' reverberates over the landscape. The final interpretation is '*Damyata*'—control (l. 418). Following the instructions to 'give' and 'sympathize', human beings have a third scenario, one that is not as dark as the last two. The concept of *Damyatta* is to have spiritual control over the self. Just as the sailor guides the boat's tiller to avoid sharp waves, the wise person steers his or her own self—eliminating anger, lust, jealousy, and other 'waves' that might rock the consciousness. It is a kind of yogic practice focused upon self-control. The goal here is to make one's passions—one's very 'heart'—beat 'obedient/To controlling hands' (ll. 421–2). Here Eliot points to the individual's wish to control a heartbeat that has been driven out of control by the concupiscence, fear, and confusion of the wasteland. This is total control, making peace out of a world that has had no peace. Eliot's words eliminate all chaos and questions, and leave the mind clear with the hand on the tiller and the boat moving calmly through the sea. Here is his new human.

Eliot presents a new paradigm, suggesting that the way to peace was within grasp all along. He suggests that if humans can kill their basest desires—if they can escape the aggressive and destructive instincts that created a wasteland of empty isolation—then there remains hope of finding peace. There are omnipresent dangers inherent in letting their passions exceed their 'control'. In the wasteland of meaningless sensuality, controlling one's passions is a never-ending task. As both the Christian and Buddhist traditions would attest, escaping suffering and falsity is not a one-time event but a daily struggle to follow a better way of living. The lust of the flesh will always be present just beneath the surface. There is an echo of Matthew Arnold's 'Dover Beach' in Eliot's line 420. Arnold's epochal poem concerned the descent of the world into anarchic destruction and Eliot's 'The sea was calm' practically mirrors the first line of 'Dover Beach'.[9] By re-invoking this context, Eliot is creating a sense of closure for the wasteland Arnold had long before identified.

The ideas of giving and sympathizing are meant to broaden people's outlooks beyond themselves (as they enter their consciousnesses). Nature herself has been awakened and has sent a message from the clouds about the solution to humanity's self-made problems. In this rejection of human institutions, human beings find release. The time for subtlety has passed. With the rains come resurrection and remonstrance. The wasteland goes beyond being a simple weather phenomenon and escaping it would require the reordering of the entire world. Humanity needs to be saved from itself, but not to create another wasteland at the first possible opportunity. The reliance upon materialism must fundamentally change to release humans from self-bondage.

Line 432 of *The Waste Land* tells humans that they have reached their journey's goal, having found an end to the whirlwind recollections of a fragmented world. The repetition of the Sanskrit words '*Datta, Dayadhvam, Damyata*', brings them back to themselves, so to speak. In the traditional tale of the thunder's speech, the gods and demons remembered what the cosmos had instructed them but humans constantly forgot and needed to be reminded (Mohanty 1994: 85–6). The last two lines are intended as a note of closure. '*Shantih shantih shantih*' is meant to indicate the attainment of peace within one's mind, returning to a realm of the soul's tranquility (Dwivedi 1984: 52–3). Though recovering the landscape may be a long and arduous road, even the sound of these words indicates that something in this world has been dramatically altered since 'The Burial of the Dead' in the first spring. The words invoke a positive desire for continued resurrection that outweighs any of the other troubles that the poem grapples with. The proclamation may be taken as a wish to begin again with a clean slate, and they hold the power to turn that desire into an eventual reality.

After the decaying of humanity, people watched as the old self was drowned in 'Death by Water' and saw the world ritually being cleansed through this baptism. This purgation of malice had a marked effect, drowning lust and false desires. With the drowning of the old humanity came an epiphany. In its wake, 'What the Thunder Said' inhabits a world that has been (and continues to be) resurrected; it is a tale of remaking the world. It brings with it a new sense of justice, demanding that the human race care for each other. Violence and indifference have been transformed into compassion and benevolence. Turmoil has turned to peace. It is this peace—'*shantih shantih shantih*'—that humans can finally cling to.

Eliot paints an ecologically unbalanced and unregenerated world in *The Waste Land* where man's complete apathy towards nature has brought about a sense of total alienation which, in turn, has resulted in a degraded and unbalanced society. It is a 'barren' life which disconcerts with its emptiness. The ecological worry and concern is such that Eliot appears to be admonishing the modern society and exhorting it to reflect and introspect upon the relationship between nature and humans, between nature and society, and even on the ecological balance and harmony within human beings on a spiritual level. Towards the end, the poet attempts to resort to religion to save the ecological crisis revealed in the poem. Eliot's ecological worries and wisdom implied in the poem is of tremendous significance in the contemporary scenario. Through his poem, Eliot tries to persuade human beings to follow the religious doctrines of 'giving', 'sympathy', and 'control' to save themselves from the plight of severe spiritual barrenness that the degradation and deterioration of nature and environment would bring in its wake.

Notes

1. According to Glen Love '[t]he word "ecocriticism" was originally coined in 1978 by William L. Rueckert, in his important essay, "Literature and Ecology: an Experiment in Ecocriticism"', in '*Et in Arcadia Ego*: Pastoral Theory Meets Ecocriticism', *Western American Literature*, vol. 27, 1992, p. 196.

2. The various definitions of the term 'alienation' can be found in Raymond Williams's *Keywords* (New York, 1976). Williams points out that the term has been used for several centuries and that some of its original meanings are still found in contemporary usage. He maintains that alienation is still used in a theological context to describe 'a state ... of being cut off, estranged from the knowledge of God'. This version, he observes, 'sometimes overlaps with a more general use, with a decisive origin in Rousseau, in which man is seen as cut off, estranged from his own original nature' (p. 30). The latter variant, thus, tends to promote ideas of 'primitivism or a cultivation of human feeling and practice against the pressures of civilization' (ibid.) to overcome alienation. Williams also emphasizes the importance of Marx's understanding of alienation, as a process anchored in 'the history of labour, in which man creates himself by creating his world, but in class-society is alienated from this essential nature by

specific forms of alienation in the division of labour, private property and the capitalist mode of production' (p. 31). From William's analysis we may deduce that Scholtmeijer's ecocritical focus on alienation is closer to Rousseau than it is to Marx.

3.   The river Thames has its own folk god, Old Father Thames, who is frequently portrayed as a bearded man, echoing the features of the traditional guardians of the City itself, Gog and Magog. His name is in recognition that the river is father to the settlements on its banks.

4.   T.S. Eliot, 'The Wasteland', *Selected Poems,* 1954 repr., London, 1982, p. 52, l. 48. All subsequent references are from the same text and the line numbers are indicated in parenthesis.

5.   In *Twilight in Delhi,* Ahmed Ali, 1940; repr., New Delhi, 2010. 'Time had reversed the order of the things, and life had been replaced by a death-in-life' (p. 241).

6.   Northrop Frye, *Anatomy of Criticism,* New York, 1969, p. 66. Frye helps us to understand this agony in his definition of anxiety as a 'terror without an object, as a condition of mind prior to being afraid *of* anything', a symptom which 'is now conceived as *Angst'*.

7.   In the *Brihadaranyaka Upanishad,* Chapter V, the Second Brahmana asked the Creator about the three principal virtues.

     On one occasion the gods, the human beings and the demons all observed self-restraint, brahmacharya (celibacy), tapasya (prayer) and austerity for the sake of gaining knowledge from the Creator. Having observed such austerity they went to Brahma, the creator, and said, 'Give us instruction.' The first group comprised the celestials, the gods, denizens of Indraloka or paradise, who enjoy all sorts of pleasures. Second, were the men of the earth, and third the demons, who were extremely cruel in their nature. To the gods he said, 'I give you instruction. Listen! Da.' He said but one word, 'Da'. 'Do you understand what I say?' 'Yes, we understand.' 'Very good! So, follow this instruction.' Then he looked to the human beings, 'Do you want instruction from me?' 'Yes!' 'Da,' he said again. 'Do you follow what I say?' 'Yes, we understand.' 'Very good! Now go and follow this instruction.' Then the demons were called and he said 'Da' to the demons also, and the demons, like the others said, 'Yes, we have understood what it is.' 'Go and follow this instruction.' To all the three he told the same thing, but the meaning was taken differently by the different groups. 'Da, Da, Da,' he said. That is all he spoke.

     The celestials, the people in paradise, are supposed to be revelling in pleasures of the sense. They are fond of enjoyment. There is no old age there. There is no sweating, no toiling, no hunger, no thirst, no drowsiness and nothing untoward as in this world. It was a life of excess and enjoyment. So the instruction to those people was Da-'*Dāmyata*'. In Sanskrit *Dāmyata* means, restrain yourself. Subdue your senses and restrain yourself from the excessive enjoyment of the senses. That was the 'Da' to the celestials.

     Human beings are defined by greed and to them 'Da' meant *Datta* or 'give in charity'. Do not keep with you more than what you need. Do not take what you have not given. Do not appropriate that which does not belong to you. All these are implied in the statement—be charitable. Charitable not only in material giving but also in disposition, in feeling, in understanding and in feeling the feelings of others. So, to the human beings the instruction was Datta or give, because they are not prepared to give.

To the cruel demons, who always insulted, injured and harmed other people, 'Da' meant *Dayadhvam* or be merciful to others. It meant to not be cruel and hard-hearted.

So, these three letters Da, Da, Da instructed three types of individuals in three different ways. All instructions were conveyed by a single word only; a single letter, but the meaning was conveyed properly to the individual groups concerned. atha hainam asurā ūcuḥ cuḥ, bravītu no bhavān iti; tebhyo haitad evākṣaram uvāca; da iti, vyajñāsiṣṭā iti, vyajñāsiṣma iti hocuḥ, dayadhvam iti na āttheti, aum iti hovāca vyajñāsiṣṭeti. tad etad evaiṣā daivī vāg anuvadati stanayitnuḥda-da, da, iti, damyata, datta, dayadhvam iti. tad etat trayaṁ śikṣet, damam, dānam, dayām iti.

These are the three great injunctions given by Prajāpati, the Creator, to three types of people. If this instruction can be followed in its spirit, then the desire, greed and anger of a personality can be sublimated by self-restraint, charity and mercy respectively.

8. <http://gita.rcmishra.com/2007/07/blog-post_04.html>

    कर्मण्येवाधिकारस्ते मा फलेषु कदाचन।
    मा कर्मफलहेतुर्भूर्मा ते सङ्गोऽस्त्वकर्मणि॑र-४७॥

9. Matthew Arnold, 'Dover Beach', 'The sea is calm to-night', <http://www.victorianweb.org/authors/arnold/writings/doverbeach.html>.

References

Adorno, Theodor W. and Max Horkheimer, *Dialectic of Enlightenment: Philosophical Fragment*, tr. John Cumming, 1944; repr., London: Verso, 1979.

Ali, Ahmed, *Twilight in Delhi*, 1940; repr., New Delhi: Rupa & Co., 2010.

Andermatt, Verena Conley, *Ecopolitics: The Environment in Post-Structuralist Thought*, London: Routledge, 1997.

Armstrong, Karen, *Buddha*, New York: Penguin, 2001.

Arnold, Matthew, 'Dover Beach', <http://www.victorianweb.org/authors/arnold/writings/doverbeach.html>.

Bennett, Michael and David W. Teague, eds., 'Urban Ecocriticism: An Introduction', in *The Nature of Cities: Ecocriticism and Urban Environments*, Tucson: University of Arizona Press, 1999.

Bersani, Leo, *The Culture of Redemption*, Cambridge: Harvard University Press, 1990.

Borg, Marcus, *Jesus and Buddha: The Parallel Sayings*, Berkeley, California: Ulysses Press, 1997.

Bradley, F.H., *Appearance and Reality: A Metaphysical Essay*, New York: Macmillan, 1893.

Brooker, Jewel Spears and Joseph Bentley, *Reading the Waste Land: Modernism and the Limits of Interpretation,* Amherst: University of Massachusetts Press, 1990.

Buell, Lawrence, 'The Ecocritical Insurgency', *New Literary History,* vol. 30, no. 3, 1999, pp. 699–712.

————, *The Environmental Imagination: Thoreau, Nature Writing, and the Formation of American Culture,* Cambridge: Belknap Press of Harvard University Press, 1995.

————, *Writing for an Endangered World: Literature, Culture, and Environment in the U.S. and Beyond,* Cambridge: Belknap Press of Harvard University Press, 2001.

Dwivedi, A.N., 'T.S. Eliot's The Waste Land', *Explicator,* vol. 43, no. 1, 1984, pp. 51–3.

Eliot, T.S., 'The Wasteland', *Selected Poems,* 1954; repr., London: Faber & Faber, 1982.

Easthope, Anthony, 'The Waste Land as a Dramatic Monologue', *English Studies: A Journal of English Language and Literature,* vol. 64, no. 4, 1983, pp. 182, 330–44.

Frye, Northrop, *Anatomy of Criticism,* New York: Atheneum, 1969.

Gifford, Terry, *Pastoral,* London: Routledge, 1999.

Glotfelty, Cheryll and Harold Fromm, eds., 'Introduction: Literary Studies in an Age of Environmental Crisis', *The Ecocriticism Reader: Landmarks in Literary Ecology,* Athens: University of Georgia Press, 1996.

Gordon, Lyndall, 'The Waste Land Manuscript', *American Literature: A Journal of Literary History, Criticism, and Bibliography,* vol. 45, no. 4, 1974, pp. 557–70.

Hassan, Ihab, 'Cities of Mind, Urban Words: The Dematerialization of Metropolis in Contemporary American Fiction', in *Literature and the Urban Experience: Essays on the City and Literature,* ed. Michael C. Jaye and Ann Chalmers Watts, New Brunswick: Rutgers University Press, 1981.

————, *Paracriticisms: Seven Speculations of the Times,* Urbana and Chicago: University of Illinois Press, 1984.

————, *The Literature of Silence: Henry Miller and Samuel Beckett,* New York: Alfred A. Knopf, 1967.

Heidegger, Martin, *The Question Concerning Technology and other Essays,* tr. William Lovitt, New York: Harper and Row, 1977.

Eliot, T.S., 'The Wasteland', Tripod.com. Accessed at <http://eliotswasteland.tripod.com>, <http://gita.rcmishra.com/2007/07/blog-post_04.html>.

Hundert, Edward J., 'Oswald Spengler: History and Metaphor, the Decline and the West', *Mosaic: A Journal for the Interdisciplinary Study of Literature,* vol.1, no. 2, 1968, pp. 103–17.

Kerridge, Richard and Neil Sammells, eds., 'Introduction', *Writing the Environment: Ecocriticism and Literature,* London and New York: Zed Books, 1998.

Lawrence, D.H., 'Why the Novel Matters', 1936, *The Norton Anthology of English Literature,* ed. M.H. Abrams, New York and London: Norton, 1986.

Litz, A. Walton, ed., *Eliot in His Time: Essays on the Occasion of the Fiftieth Anniversary of The Waste Land,* Princeton, New Jersey: Princeton University Press, 1973.

Love, Glen, 'Et in Arcadia Ego: Pastoral Theory Meets Ecocriticism', *Western American Literature,* vol. 27, 1992, pp. 195–207.

Marx, Leo, *The Machine in the Garden: Technology and the Pastoral Ideal In America*, 1964; repr., Oxford: Oxford University Press, 1967.

Miller, Henry, *The Air-Conditioned Nightmare,* 1945; repr., New York: New Directions, 1970.

———, *Tropic of Cancer*, 1934; repr., London: Flamingo, 1993.

———, *The World of Lawrence: A Passionate Appreciation*, ed. Evelyn J. Hinz and John J. Teunissen, Santa Barbara: Capra, 1980.

Miller, James E. Jr., *T.S. Eliot's Personal Waste Land: Exorcism of the Demons*, University Park, Pennsylvania: Pennsylvania State University Press, 1977.

Mohanty, Bindu, 'The Ordering of the Sanskrit Words in T.S. Eliot's *The Waste Land*', *ANQ: A Quarterly Journal of Short Articles, Notes, and Reviews*, vol. 7, no. 2, 1994, pp. 84–8.

Nichols, James R., 'Shilly Shandies Lawrence Durell Eighteenth Century Rationalist', in *Lawrence Durell: Comprehending the Whole*, ed. Julius Rowan Raper, Columbia: University of Missouri Press, 1995.

Phillips, Dana, 'Introduction', in *The Truth of Ecology: Nature, Culture, and Literature in America*, Oxford: Oxford University Press, 2003.

Pike, Burton, *The Image of the City in Modern Literature*, Princeton: Princeton University Press, 1981.

Pogue, Robert Harrison, *Forests: The Shadow of Civilization*, Chicago: University of Chicago Press, 1992.

Scholtmeijer, Marian, *Animal Victims in Modern Fiction: From Sanctity to Sacrifice,* Toronto: University of Toronto Press, 1993.

Sorum, Eve, 'Masochistic Modernisms: A Reading of Eliot and Woolf', *Journal of Modern Literature*, vol. 28, no. 3, 2005, pp. 25–43.

Spanos, William V., 'Repetition in The Waste Land: A Phenomenological Destruction', *Boundary 2: An International Journal of Literature and Culture*, vol. 7, no. 3, 1979, pp. 225–85.

The NIV Study Bible, Kenneth L. Barker, gen. ed. Grand Rapids, Michigan: Zondervan Publishing Co., 1995.

Thormählen, Marianne, 'Dry Bones Can Harm No One: Ezekiel XXXVII in The Waste Land V and "Ash-Wednesday" II', *English Studies: A Journal of English Language and Literature*, vol. 65, no. 1, 1984, pp. 39–47, 189.

Tamplin, Ronald, *The Tempest* and *The Waste Land, American Literature: A Journal of Literary History, Criticism, and Bibliography*, vol. 39, no. 3, 1967, pp. 352–72.

Ward, David, *T.S. Eliot Between Two Worlds: A Reading of T. S. Eliot's Poetry and Plays*, London: Routledge and Kegan Paul, 1973.

Weston, Jessie L., *From Ritual to Romance*, Princeton, New Jersey: Princeton University Press, 1993.

Williams, Raymond, *Keywords: A Vocabulary of Culture and Society*, New York: Oxford University Press, 1976.

———, *The Country and the City*, 1973; repr., London: Hogarth Press, 1985.

Willis, Roy, ed., *Signifying Animals: Human Meaning in the Natural World*, London: Unwin Hyman, 1990.

5

Magic Realism as Ecocriticism

An Analysis of Salman Rushdie's
Haroun and the Sea of Stories

NISHA TIWARI

T HE CONTENTION OF 'truth(s)' remains one of the foremost concerns in literary criticism and theory from the twentieth century onwards. Writers and critics have experimented with various literary devices and theories in order to destabilize the notion of 'truth' and uncover the discourses invested in the construction of normative truth. This essay looks at two such literary categories, a literary theory (ecocriticism) and a literary device (magic realism) in order to delineate the symbiotic possibilities between the two. While ecocriticism is preoccupied with unearthing human-centric discourses on nature, magic realism as a narrative technique reconfigures the notions of truth and reality vis-à-vis alternate worlds and voices. It is precisely at the intersection of these two categories that I situate the premise of this essay.

Divided into three sections, the first section of the essay explores and establishes the contemporary definitions and descriptions of the two aforementioned categories. The second section streamlines the overlapping concerns of magic realism and ecocriticism. The third section contextualizes the overlap in these two discourses to analyse Salman Rushdie's novel *Haroun and the Sea of Stories* (1990) for an effective application of the same. The objective will be to explore the manner in which the narrative device of magic realism, deployed in the novel, reflects upon the issues pertaining to ecocriticism.

Ever since its emergence in the 1970s, ecocriticism is regarded 'as a form of literary and cultural critique that uses the environment as its frame of reference' (Vital 2008: 87). Cheryl Glotfelty, a renowned ecocritic, states in her essay, 'What is Ecocriticism?':

Simply defined, ecocriticism is the study of the relationship between literature and the physical environment.... Ecocriticism takes as its subject the interconnections between nature and culture, specifically the cultural artifacts, language and literature. As a critical stance, it has one foot in literature and the other on land; as a theoretical discourse, it negotiates between the human and the non-human. (2012)

In Glotfelty's definition of ecocriticism there is an obvious attempt to bridge the binary opposition between nature and culture. Similarly, Greg Garrard, in what he calls the 'widest definition of ecocriticism', states that it is 'the study of the relationship of the human and the non-human, throughout human cultural history and entailing critical analysis of the term "human" itself' (2004: 5). He deems it 'an avowedly political mode of analysis', where the cultural analysis gets interwoven with a '"green" moral and political agenda' (2004: 3). He further states that 'As ecocritics seek to offer a truly transformative discourse, enabling us to analyse and criticize the world in which we live, attention is increasingly given to the broad range of cultural processes and products in which, and through which, the complex negotiations of nature and culture take place' (2004: 4). What is central to the foregrounding of ecocriticism in these definitions (Vital, Glotfelty, and Garrard) is the delineation of the human configurations of nature.

However, ecocriticism, until recently, has been accused of acknowledging only those texts, which mention ecological and environmental aspects in tangible forms (viz., empirical presence of animate non-human beings like trees, animals, etc.) and excluding those literary works, which foregrounded the human perception of the same. This opposition between the so-called 'authentic', 'realistic' or 'pure' description of the ecosphere, which was deemed to be objective, and the articulation of the human subject's perception of the environment (termed 'nature') intensified to such an extent that some ecocritics have argued that, 'there is no such thing as nature' (Laurence Coupe as qtd. in Benito et al. 2009: 196). These critics contend that only the realist narrative mode adopted in literature works in tandem with the concerns of ecocriticism as it portrays nature, if at all, with authenticity. The conventions built around ecocritical studies have targeted the factual accuracy in describing the ecosystem in literary texts. Glotfelty's argument is a case in point. She states that:

If your knowledge of the outside world were limited to what you could infer from the major publications of the literary profession, you would quickly discern that race, class and gender were the hot topics of the later twentieth century, but you would never suspect that the earth's life support systems were under stress. Indeed, you might never know there was an earth at all. In contrast, if you were to scan the newspaper headlines of the same period, you would learn of oil spills, lead and asbestos poisoning, toxic waste contaminations, extinction of species at an unprecedented rate. (2012: xvi)

Glotfelty, like many other ecocritics, seeks to obtain a direct reference to the ecological crisis in literary texts. This attitude has, more often than not, led to a deliberate dismissal of the ecological significance of texts, which employ anti-realist or counter-realist techniques of narration. In doing so, the realm of ecocritical studies commits the error of overlooking a vast section of contemporary literature, which involves postmodern (read anti-realist) narrative strategies for a large part. The pervading influence of poststructuralism used by these counter-realist narrative strategies in their interrogation of realism as trustworthy or 'natural' has worked tangentially to this erstwhile assumption of what constitutes the analytical trope for ecocritical studies. The argument of this essay stems from precisely this juncture where the need to broaden the critical parameters of ecocriticism pushes the envelope in order to encompass the contemporary postmodern literary landscape within its realm of analysis.

Lawrence Buell, an eminent scholar in the field of ecocriticism, comments on the role of culture, imagination and the human value system as some of the important factors that have led to environmental degradation. According to him, 'many non-humanists would agree—often more readily than doubt-prone-humanists—that issues of vision, value, culture, and imagination are keys to today's environmental crises at least as fundamental as scientific research, technological know-how, and legislative regulation' (2005: 6). In holding these building blocks of human civilization as key factors in the degradation of non-human entities, Buell's statement calls for a reassessment of the role of culture in shaping an individual, a community and even a civilization's view and perspective on nature. In the process, man-made culture as a dominating force over nature also comes under scrutiny.

The ecocritic Garrard calls for a close examination of the manner in which '"nature" is always in some ways culturally constructed' (2004: 10). Lawrence Buell prefers the term 'environmental criticism' instead and adds that this is, in fact, 'a myth of mutual constructionism: of physical environment (both natural and human-built) shaping in some measure the cultures that refashion it' (qtd. in Garrard 2004: 10). Consequently, the nature and intent of man's reason/rational faculty, which has earned him a 'privileged' status on earth is interrogated, whereby his 'natural legacy' over the ecological sphere is problematized. It is in this respect that Buell assesses the importance of the recent collaborative enterprise between contemporary postmodern theory and ecocriticism, which has resulted in 'de-privileging the human subject', and, thus, questioning the assumptions of anthropocentrism and androcentrism (2005: 10).

These concepts assume that the human rationale and explanation of the world (which are essentially male dominated) is the only possible and valid explanation of the world and nature around us. In other words, the postmodern anti-realist or counter-realist narratorial stance facilitates the interrogation of androcentric 'realist' accounts of the environment. Buell's conclusions open up new avenues to examine postmodern modes of narration for their relevance to ecocritical studies. It also highlights why magic realism is one of the most popular narrative modes among postmodern-postcolonial writers.[1]

Critics have offered a wide range of definitions of magic realism. Franz Roh describes magic realism as a 'magical insight into the hardly interpreted piece of reality' (Roh qtd. in Bényei 1997: 152). As the oxymoronic aspect of the term magic and realism suggests, it is a combination of two presumably opposing dimensions into one narrative mode. The motive behind such an alliance is to portray an experience of assimilation and illusion as opposed to a culture that operates primarily on the principle of binary opposition, subsequently subjugating, marginalizing, and obliterating cultural categories and experiences. Tamás Bényei states:

'Magic realism' is a mode of writing that responds to a particular cultural situation (marginalization, multiculturalism, displacement and so forth). Most often, perhaps, it is seen as the 'place' where postmodernism and postcolonialism overlap or interpenetrate' (1997: 150). One can argue that the destabilizing and contesting impulse of magic realism allows writers as well as readers to react to, resist and assert their own experiences against the overpowering and normative narratives of the dominant discourse—be it the monolithic realism of the Western discourse, or racialized/colonized structures of power. Maggie Ann Bower writes: 'much magic realism has originated in many of the postcolonial countries that are battling against the influence of their previous colonial rulers'. (2004: 31)

Within the corpus of its narration magic realism encompasses the imaginary, the fantastical, the fabulous, and the supernatural not in opposition to the traditional Western realism, but rather as simultaneous parts. These aspects coalesce into an entire human experience which also encapsulates the community. In this light, magic realism can be seen as a mode of narration that conjoins the counter-realist and anti-realist aspects under its rubric. It constructs a narrative built into the rubric of a community or a tradition, thus, providing an insight into the human understanding of nature vis-à-vis their communitarian interests.

According to Brenda Cooper, magic realism strives to 'capture the paradox of the unity of opposites' and in the process contests polarities (Cooper qtd. in Nayar 2008: 235). These texts, according to Cooper, exist between the 'extremes of time and space' (Cooper qtd. in Nayar 2008: 235). It is a space where the pre-colonial past and the post-industrial present can coexist. Furthermore, Pramod Nayar extrapolates this definition into the postcolonial situation stating that magic realist texts 'embody points of transition in postcolonial society where the two forms battle for power in contemporary geopolitics' (2008: 235–6). In doing so, these texts inevitably re-evaluate their immediate cultural perceptions towards nature vis-à-vis the inherited cultural perceptions of their native traditions (in the form of myths, rituals and beliefs) and the aftermath of the industrial or colonial intervention. In relation to Third World texts, Frederic Jameson points out that, 'the story of the private individual destiny is always an allegory of the embattled situation of the public third world culture and society' (Jameson qtd. in Ghosh-Schellhorn 1999: 30).

In comparing the definitions of the categories of ecocriticism and magic realism, one cannot overlook the fact that they interlace their use of culture as a primary phenomenon of examination. The interconnections between the two have of late drawn the attention, of some literary scholars. Katherine Hayles celebrates the inclusion of the anti-realist postmodern devices into the scrutiny of the ecocritical eye. Hayles states that the use of postmodern devices in contemporary literature strongly implies the idea 'that what has always been thought of as the essential, unvarying components of human experience are not natural facts of life but social constructions' (Hayles qtd. in Benito et al. 2009: 198).

In the essay, 'Of a Magical Nature: The Environmental Unconscious', Jesus Benito et al. offer a detailed discussion of the manner in which magic realism and ecocriticism converge. According to them, there are roughly three broad points of interconnection between the two categories. First, in transgressing the confines of the realist epistemology, magic realism facilitates the interrogations and subsequent deconstruction of the traditional binaries of human versus non-human and nature versus culture. Second, they argue that it also throws light on the usually implicit and veiled strategic relations between material practices (late capitalism, globalization, social injustice, etc.), spiritual and ethical issues, and environmental degradation (Benito et al. 2009: 194). Thus, it empowers the counter-narrative framework with the tools of inclusion, assimilation and conglomeration, which then prepares the backdrop for the contestation of normative truths and practices regarding the human-centric perceptions of nature and its role. Yvonne Hammer observes:

In fictions which form the basis for ecocriticism authors may create similar narrative spaces of resistance to encode representations of ecological malpractice which are enacted upon indigenous people by an invasive non-indigenous presence.... The convergent aims of dual interrogative frames—ecocriticism and magic realism—also provide contradictory grounds for the representation of the marginal positions because indigenous perspectives are represented through the lens of non-indigenous agents. (2008: 41)

Third, magic realism provides functional alternative spaces to engage, interrogate, and experiment with reality in order to explore and negotiate more feasible solutions to the immediate ecological existential crises (Benito et al. 2009: 194–5). This provision of alternative spaces for interrogation, discursion, and reflection allows opportunities for ecocritical reflection of cultures vis-à-vis the ecosystem.

In the light of these parallels between the two categories, I examine Salman Rushdie's novel *Haroun and the Sea of Stories* for its use of magic realism as a narrative device in order to deal with cultural and political themes, which overlap with the concerns of ecocriticism. In the process, I will also analyse how such a problematization of the dominant discourse implicitly constitutes a strong ecocritical statement. The novel, through the use of magic realism, problematizes the monolithic truth by juxtaposing it with other versions of the experience. Andrew Teverson aptly sums up the novel as, 'the adventures of a central hero who begins the tale in a comfortable domestic environment to visit a fantasy world full of peculiarities and marvels—though strangely parallel to his or her own world—then returns home to find that his or her understanding of the home world has been clarified' (2001: 454). *Haroun and the Sea of Stories* juxtaposes the dominant normative experience of the 'rational' human existence with the world of imagination. As a result of this juxtaposition one finds an alternative perspective, which allows the reader not only to doubt the human enterprise of reason but also to question the validity of its privileged status in society.

Throughout the novel, one finds the author constantly complimenting the human order of the world with an alternate unbound trope of nature, which exists in a wild, confusing form yet has a harmonious ring to it. This alternate trope allows the reader to question the hitherto inhabited and rationally ordered human world, which from the vantage point of its narrator and through Haroun's eyes is shown to be incomplete in its assimilation of the lived experience. When regarded within this framework of magic realism and its ecocritical potential, Salman Rushdie's novel *Haroun and the Sea of Stories*, as the title suggests, presents the protagonist Haroun with what can be described in Hammer's term as the 'nonindigenous eco-warrior' (2008: 41). Hammer further observes that, 'Representations of childhood agency and voice are strongly supported by the eco-warrior protagonists who act as catalysts for environmental justice and indigenous rights' (2008: 42). Haroun is a child protagonist from Alifbay whose innocence allows him to enter the indigenous and ecological realm known as the Land of Kahani without the risk of superimposing the patriarchal normative discourse into its indigenous culture. Thus, it facilitates the first aim of ecocriticism, viz., its 'hope . . . to replace anthropocentrism by ecocentrism' (Abrahams and Harpham 2009: 83).

Suchismita Sen states, 'Haroun provides us with a child's-eye view of a world that urban Indians will have little difficulty in recognizing as their own childhood environment and homeland' (1995: 662). The non-indigenous world of Alifbay in the novel is mimetically and nostalgically described as urbanized, industrialized and mechanized. Rushdie's novel opens by taking the readers into the country of Alifbay where black smoke poured out of the factories 'sadness was actually manufactured: one of the many damages that the overrated scientific "progress" of man has wreaked upon the earth' (1990: 21). Hence, the city of Alifbay becomes 'a potent political allegory that confronts pertinent contemporary issues ... [like] the pollution of the environment by irresponsible multinational corporations' (Teverson 2001: 454). Therefore, Rushdie foregrounds Alifbay as a land fraught with the crisis of modernity, which manifests itself through environmental degradation.

While speaking about postcolonial (African) ecocriticism, Anthony Vital highlights that it 'engages in debating what a society's assigning of significance to nature (in varieties of cultural products) reveals about both its present and past' (2008: 87). According to Vital, it allows us to interrogate within the postcolonial indigenous landscape the manner in which modernity 'transforms human relations with nature and, as a result, the impact of societies on natural environments ...' (2008: 87). In the world that Mr Sengupta and the likes of him inhabit in this novel, there is a constant derision of anything that poses a threat to the supremacy of the human reason, which is compulsively considered to be at the apex of all 'structures' that rule the planet. The threat to this order comes from Rashid's stories, which get scorned by the rationalist Sengupta as 'full of make-believe, so there is no room for facts' (Rushdie 1990: 22). The selfish utilitarian interests that override human actions are best seen in Sengupta's comment: 'What's the use of the stories that aren't even true?' (Rushdie 1990: 20). This technology-driven industrialized town of Alifbay suffers a soot-ridden despaired existence which, as the author suggests, is a result of the monolithic rationality that dominates the lives of its inhabitants.

As opposed to this, Rashid's stories offer the people of Alifbay an insight into something lacking in their rational yet incomplete and incoherent existence. It opens a world of imagination and overwhelming emotions, which are otherwise, absent in the lives of the people of Alifbay. Rashid's stories are the only hope-inducing element in their arid lives. It is also significant that these stories, which find their home in Rashid, or the Shah of Blah's stories, as one later comes to know, flow from 'the great Story Sea' (Rushdie 1990: 17) in a different world (the Land of Gup) where nature, as Rushdie portrays it, exists in all its variety, abundance, and an all-inclusive harmonious confusion. The 'Ocean of Notion' filled with the 'story waters' is described as 'much more than a storeroom of yarns. It is not dead but alive' (Rushdie 1990: 72). It is a world of the non-human, the fantastical—the world of hoopoe (the bird), water genies, plentimaw fishes, walruses, etc. All of these cohabit harmoniously in the old land of Kahani in the lap of nature and are projected in stark contrast to the 'mournful sea full of glumfish' (Rushdie 1990: 15). It is through the use of magic realism that Rushdie encourages the 'interaction (intercourse) between the sensate and the non-sensate, the animate and the inanimate', thus causing 'an interpenetration of orders' (Benito et al. 2009: 198).

The sad city with its 'black smoke', 'mighty factories' and 'ruined building', is presented as an aftermath of Alifbay's fateful appropriation of the Western strategies of progress and development. Hammer argues that the use of magic realism to depict an ecologically inclusive realm as opposed to the progressive human world serves to underline the distinct practices of modernity, as witnessed in the industrial city of Alifbay, with its 'characterizations of western attitudes or environmental practices which disregard the value of wilderness areas and indigenous culture' (2008: 43). The author offers the trope of the old land of Kahani in order to demonstrate how nature in its wild, unregulated existence can achieve peace, which the human world fails to acquire through order, regulation, and control.

Rushdie's criticism of the regimentation (in this case, the State) is seen in the caricature of Mr Buttoo, the military dictator of the 'Valley of K' (an allusion to the Kashmir valley) and his rejection by the valley as is seen in the wild behaviour of the otherwise calm Dull Lake (an allusion to the Dal Lake of Kashmir). The ecosphere of the 'Valley of K' is shown to be warm as the helping nature of Mr Buttoo, and the warmth of the Dull Lake towards Haroun and Rashid. The lake resists any attempt to be overpowered or controlled by any one power. The natural world of the Kashmir valley— alias the Valley of K—has been affected by the oppressive regime and the territorial violence inflicted upon it by the State as embodied in the figure of the dictator Mr Buttoo. The cultural perception of the land corroborates with its ecological condition. 'Kache-mer' (the land that hides the sea) gets violated in order to become 'Kosh-mar' (which means nightmare). In fact, the violence has not only affected the lakes but also the spirit of the common multitudes. Hammer states:

These representations of the consequences of environmental and cultural abuse construct ideological confluence between magic realist ideologies and ecocritical frames. Each narrative establishes a strong narrator presence—a dominant representative voice—which speaks from margins to educate and inform the readers, to privilege minority culture, and finally give voice to other ways of perceiving the world ... the evident environmental justice themes [that] are depicted in each quest affirm indigenous voices, adolescent quest structures encode representations of agency that centre narrative development in the magical empowerment of child/adolescent protagonists.... (2008: 44)

The novel deploys Haroun, the adolescent protagonist, as an agency to enlighten the readers to not just the indigenous voices but also to the innate feature of plurality that they embody in their harmonious and dialogic interaction with nature. The assimilative and inclusive character of the land of Kahani, and the Gupees is in stark contrast to the tragic and forced marginalization and alienation of the 'natives' (Kashmiris) within the Valley of K. The apparent hostility of the Dull Lake towards the Military Commander, Mr Buttoo acts as a foil to the palpable proximity of the Gupees to their story sea. Haroun partakes of this experience when he drinks from the story waters. His participation in rescuing the 'Ocean of Notions' at a later stage in the novel demonstrates his comprehension of the significance of this experience.

One of the important objectives often associated with the alliance between magic realism and ecocriticism is that an 'alignment between the indigenous perspective and the enviro-cultural preservation is consistently affirmed [and] . . . the anthropocentric views of the environment are undermined' (Hammer 2008: 43). In *Haroun and the Sea of Stories*, Rushdie loops in culture and nature into one through the device of magic realism dismantling the conventional domination of culture over nature by portraying the two to be intertwined in his novel. This critique of binaries (nature versus culture, man versus beast) is the second prominent concern of ecocriticism (Abrahams and Harpham 2009: 83). Also, as is evident in the novel, while strongly advocating inclusion and plurality, Rushdie also expresses his disapproval of the policies of exclusion and control. Teverson argues:

. . . the story sea as an image of Rushdie's hybrid sources comes to reflect one of the dominant arguments present in the plot of Haroun—that the establishment of strict and impenetrable boundaries between cultures gives a false impression of the 'purity' of each culture and prevents cultural groups from discovering that their respective social narratives provide as much of a basis for dialogue and communication as they do for segregation and separation. (2001: 458)

The novel also projects the sinister world collapsing under the threat of permanent dominance of reason in the annexation of the world of Gup by the land of Chup. In his ominous obsession with order and control, the arch villain Khattam Shud who rules the land of Chup, endangers nature as he plans to poison the ocean, which is the life rendering source, to the land of Gup. Coincidentally, he resembles Mr Sengupta, in his apparent hatred for stories and championing of utilitarian and normative choices. Khattam Shud ambitiously states his reason for hating stories: 'They (i.e. all worlds) are all there to be Ruled. And inside every single story, inside every Stream in the Ocean, there lies a world, a story world that I cannot Rule at all. And that is the reason why' (1990: 161). Rushdie's underhand attack on this categorization of reason and imagination is depicted in the split in the body and the shadow of the Chupwallahs where the ecological crisis is portrayed in terms of eternal night and icelands. Khattam Shud wages a war in order to annex the sunlight that falls on the Land of Gup. The author implies that imagination is as important to human life as water to earth and the destruction of either leads to the road to self-annihilation.

The novel ends with a peaceful resolution between the Guppees and the Chupwallahs—a resolution of the battle between imagination and reason—amidst the twilight and the clean and colourful story waters. Ultimately, imagination is restored not only to the land of Kahani but also to the Valley of K and the town of Alifbay when Haroun realizes the importance of imagination to one's existence. Thus, in the end what saves Haroun and the Ocean of Stories 'is not technology or science-fictive strategies, but a bottle of "wish-water of pure-fairytale variety"' (Mukherjee 2009: 194). Ultimately, the harmonious existence in the land of Gup is depicted in a scene of twilight where the setting sun is followed by a moonrise, unlike the earlier factional division between the two kingdoms of the sun and the moon. Rushdie seems to suggest that peace can be achieved only when mankind casts away its ambition to control and manipulate phenomena like nature or imagination to suit its vested interests. This appears to coincide with the primary objective of ecocriticism which 'maintain[s] that the human relationship to the non-human world is not one of mastery, but of stewardship, and which recognize[s] the deep human need for the natural world as something to be enjoyed for its own sake, as well as the moral responsibility of human beings to maintain and transmit a livable, diverse and enjoyable world to their posterity' (Abrahams and Harpham 2009: 84). Thus, as the novel demonstrates in the case of the people of Alifbay and the land of Chup, peace and harmony are achieved when nature is considered to be a part of the community. In contrast to this, it is only when mankind divorces itself from the environment, perceives it as 'the Other' and tries to control it, that it wreaks havoc not only on the environment but also upon its own existence. In this context, Cheryl Glotfelty asserts:

In most literary theory 'the world' is synonymous with society—the social sphere. Ecocriticism expands the notion of 'the world' to include the entire ecosphere. If we agree with Barry Commoner's first law of ecology, that 'Everything is connected to everything else,' we must conclude that literature does not float above the material world in some aesthetic ether, but, rather, plays a part in an immensely complex global system, in which energy, matter, and ideas interact. (2012)

Environmentalists also maintain that the solution lies not in creating new codes of conduct, rather as Abrahams and Harpham put it, 'in identifying and developing those strands in the human centered religion, philosophy and ethics' which help in assimilating a harmonious relation with the environment (2009: 84). Therefore, one sees 'a growing interest among environmentalists in "primitive" cultures, as well as Hindu, Buddhist and other religions and civilizations that lack the Western opposition between humanity and nature and do not assign to human beings autonomy over the non-human world' (Abraham and Harpham 2009: 84). Rushdie's use of the magic realist narration serves this purpose, as it helps him to bank on his native oral traditions of *Arabian Nights* as well as *Kathasaritasagara* (Devadawson 2009: 177). His passionate advocacy for the telling of stories 'from all over the world' (Rushdie 1990: 21), which is one of the thematic concerns of the text, is a significant effort towards reinterpretation of truths and realities in the pluralities of stories and oral traditions. Rushdie's use of magic realism appears to be more than just a popular postcolonial narrative device; it becomes a medium to make serious statements about the exploitation inherent in the contemporary phenomenon of capitalism, globalization and social progress.

Ecofeminist Vandana Shiva discusses the aftermath of colonization and the havoc it wreaked upon the sustenance of both nature and women. She posits the 'feminine principle', which looks at the points of connection between women and nature, and its significance for the humankind. Shiva states:

With the violation of nature is linked the violation and marginalisation of women, especially in the Third World. All ecological societies ... whose life is organized around the principle of sustainability and the reproduction of life in all its richness, also embody the feminine principle. The devaluation of subsistence, or rather sustenance economies, based on harmony between nature's work, women's work and man's work has created the various forms of ethnic and cultural crises that plague our world today. (1989: 43–4)

In this context, it is important to study the manner in which the novel uses the female presence. In each of the three worlds, the cultural and ecological crises can be linked to the temporary absence of women—as in case of Rashid's wife, Soraya's elopement, or the abduction of Princess Baatcheat from the Land of Gup—or a permanent one, as in the case of the Valley of K. This absence of a female figure carries within it a potent possibility of sterility. For example, in the town of Alifbay, Soraya's elopement causes Rashid's inability to produce stories. Although, Mrs Sengupta is around, she is shown to be unable to produce any children, and therefore, sterile. It is important to note that in both the cases of Soraya and Princess Baatcheat, the danger is caused by the monolithic, normative, dominating, and rational structure epitomized by Mr Sengupta and Khattam Shud. Subsequently, their absence causes a crisis of sustenance in Alifbay and the Land of Gup, respectively. In this regard, the women can be said to embody what Shiva calls the 'feminine principle' whose loss is threatened by an overpowering presence of the rationalist and utilitarian discourse. It is only with the return of Princess Baatcheat and Soraya, that the restoration of peace takes place.

Magic realist narratives have often been accused of 'limit[ing] the development of a gential capacities' of the eco-warrior by using the strategy of displacement that then restricts the experience of ecological and indigenous interactions to merely an adventure (Huggan qtd. in Hammer 2008: 44). Rushdie's novel stands out in the manner in which the three worlds—Alifbay and lands of Gup and Chup—are shown to be interdependent. Haroun's 'adventure of Kahani' then helps him restore Rashid's storytelling powers, and more importantly, helps him in his attempts to 'unmechanize' the life of Alifbay.

Thus, Salman Rushdie's novel *Haroun and the Sea of Stories* can be read as a strong statement on the relationship of man and his cultures with nature. It can also be concluded that such an inclusive and informed demonstration of this relation is possible due to the author's use of magic realism as a narrative mode in his work. In this respect, magic realism offers a unique trope that enables an active negotiation of nature as a constitutive part of the human culture, and vice versa. It also implies that any phenomenon or change in one is bound to affect the other. The narrative mode of magic realism, therefore, works in tandem with the objective of ecocriticism as it contests and re-perspectivizes the 'realism' with which human civilization rationalizes and normatizes its imposition upon nature. In addition, it also allows postcolonial narratives to combine pre-colonial traditions to examine their postcolonial situations. The current theoretical contexts of postmodernism and post-structuralism make it possible to deploy ecocriticism in the coordinates of magic realism and postcolonial literature.

This essay attempted to capture the interweaving concerns of the postmodern magic realist texts and the postulates of the very recent discipline of ecocriticism. In the process, the attempt was to highlight the need for ecocriticism to delineate the subtexts of counter-realist literary forms in order to explore the profound, albeit veiled, perceptions and articulations of the environment. In doing so, ecocriticism can enrich itself with the tools to explore into the vast, varied, and ever-increasing landscape of contemporary literature.

Note

1. The canon of magic-realist literature comprises of authors like Gabriel Garcia Marquez (*One Hundred Years of Solitude*, 1967); Salman Rushdie (*Midnight's Children*, 1981); Isabelle Allende's *The House of Spirits*, 1982); Angle Carter (*Night at the Circus*, 1984); Jeanette Winterson (*The Passion*, 1987; *Sexing the Cherry*, 1989) and Yann Martel (*The Life of Pi*, 2001) among others.

References

Abrahams, M.H. and Geoffrey Harpham, 'Ecocriticism', *A Handbook of Literary Terms*, New Delhi: Cengage, 2009, pp. 81–5.

Ann Bowers, Maggie, 'Locations of Magic(al) Realism', *Magic(al) Realism: The New Critical Idiom*, New York: Routledge, 2004, pp. 31–62.

Benito, Jesús, Ana Ma Manzanas and Bego a Simal, 'Of a Magical Nature: The Environmental Unconscious', *Uncertain Mirrors: Magical Realisms in US Ethnic Literatures*, New York: Rodopi, 2009, pp. 193–238.

Bényei, Tamás, 'Rereading 'Magic Realism', *Hungarian Journal of English and American Studies*, vol. 3, no. 1, 1997, pp. 41–7.

Buell, Lawrence, 'The Emergence of Environmental Criticism', *The Future of Environmental Criticism: Environmental Crisis and Literary Imagination*, Oxford: Blackwell, 2005, pp. 1–28.

Devadawson, Christel, 'The Limits of Fantasy: Haroun and the Sea of Stories', in *Rushdie the Novelist: from Grimus to The Enchantress of Florence*, ed. Meenakshi Bharat, New Delhi: Pencraft, 2009, pp. 177–84.

Garrard, Greg, 'Beginnings: Pollution', *Ecocriticism*, New York: Routledge, 2004, pp. 1–15.

Ghosh-Schellhorn, Martina, 'Spaced in Between: Transitional Identity', in *Borderlands: Negotiating Boundaries in Post Colonial Writing*, ed. Monika Reif-Hülser, Amsterdam: Rodopi, 1999, pp. 29–42.

Glotfelty, Cheryl, 'What is Ecocriticism?' , <http://www.asle.org/site/resources/ecocriticallibrary/intro/defining/glotfelty/>, accessed on 31 October 2012.

Hammer, Yvonne, 'Conflicting Ideologies in Three Magic Realist Children's Novels by Isabel Allende', *Explorations into Children's Literature*, vol. 18, no. 2, 2008.

Mukherjee, Meenakshi, 'Haroun and the Sea of Stories: Fantasy or Fable?', in *Rushdie the Novelist: From Grimus to The Enchantress of Florence*, ed. Meenakshi Bharat, New Delhi: Pencraft, 2009, pp. 185–98.

Nayar, Pramod K., 'Form: Magic Realism', *Postcolonial Literature: An Introduction*, New Delhi: Pearson, 2008, pp. 235–8.

Rushdie, Salman, *Haroun and the Sea of Stories*, New Delhi: Penguin, 1990.

Sen, Suchismita, 'Memory, Language, and Society in Salman Rushdie's "Haroun and the Sea of Stories",' *Contemporary Literature*, vol. 36, no. 4, Winter 1995, pp. 654–75.

Shiva, Vandana, 'Women in Nature', *Staying Alive: Women, Ecology and Development*, New Delhi: Kali for Women, 1989, pp. 38–54.

Teverson, Andrew S., 'Fairy Tale Politics: Free Speech and Multiculturalism in Haroun and The Sea of Stories', *Twentieth Century Literature*, vol. 47, no. 4, Winter 2001, pp. 444–66.

Vital, Antony, 'Toward an African Ecocriticism: Postcolonialism, Ecology and "Life & Times of Michael K."', *Research in African Literatures*, vol. 39, no.1, Spring 2008, pp. 87–106.

6

Quo Vadis Human Civilization?

The Ecopoetics of Thoreau's *Walden* in the Anthropocene

SHIVANI JHA

'I desire to speak somewhere without bounds; like a man in a waking moment, to men in their waking moments.'

— THOREAU, *Walden*

An ecological humanism would restore appropriate humility ... emphasizing cooperative participation within the community of planetary life.

—*Louise Westling, PMLA*, 1999

IN ORDER TO UNDERSTAND the relevance of the ecopoetics of Thoreau's *Walden*, it is necessary to understand the contemporary ecological scenario. There have been five mass extinctions on earth so far taking a huge toll on biodiversity. It is increasingly being perceived by the scientific community that the human race has entered the sixth mass extinction phase (Wagler 2011: 78) with threatening unknown ecological and evolutionary consequences (Jeremy Jackson as qtd by Wagler, 2011). Environmental scientists C. Kueffer and C.N. Kaiser-Bunbury believe that whereas in the past conservation of biodiversity meant restricting human interference with the environment, in the altered scenario of multiple threats to the historical biodiversity, arising even for protected areas, an early and long lasting active human intervention on behalf of the environment has become an imperative. In order to undo the damage done to the ecology so far these scientists recommend a four step human intervention: '(1) removing existing threats; (2) preventing further impacts; (3) reinforcing remnant populations, which are often too small to be viable; and (4) restoring vital ecological interactions and processes' (2014: 133).

This essay is based on the premise that in the Anthropocene Thoreau's text *Walden* as an ecological treatise, has become more pertinent than ever, for not only questioning the anthropocentric attitude of the humans but for pointing the way ahead for a harmonious cohabitation of the human and the non-human world. [The term 'Anthropocene' was coined in 2002 by Nobel Laureate Paul Crutzen to describe the current, modern epoch of human–induced environmental changes (Coombs 2014).] Tracing the origin of the human species, Anthropologist Gisli Palsson (1996) has charted three different stages in its evolution and development marked by: communalism, orientalism and paternalism respectively. In the 'Communalist phase' humans live in harmony with the environment and the non-human world. Activities of hunting are conducted in the spirit of love and respect. In the 'Orientalist phase' there is a shift in the ethos and the feelings of harmony, love, and respect are replaced by that of domination and exploitation. In the 'paternalistic phase' the orientalist ethos gives way to that of protection. Henry David Thoreau's *Walden* belongs to the 'Paternalistic' phase of protection of the environment and the non-human world.

In the face of the extensive damage done to ecology, which cannot be easily undone and the loss of much of the pristine glory of the world and of the diversity in flora and fauna, *Walden* is a text which through its principles of environmental ethics and its registration of the gross anthropocentric changes in the nineteenth-century America reaches out not only to the American preservationist ethos but to that of the world at large. In keeping with the aim of ecocriticism, the restoration of 'ecological humanism', I thus approach Thoreau's celebrated work *Walden* as a site of environmental-ethical reflection and a critique of anthropocentrism.

Before moving on to the discussion of *Walden*, I would like to dwell a little on the term 'ecological humanism'. It was first used by Louise Westling while responding to a call by the *PML* in 1999 for comments on the importance and scope of environmental literature and ecological literary criticism. In her letter, Westling emphasized upon the need for a 'paradigm shift' in the attitude of the developed world keeping in view the global environmental crises. A significant change that she recommended was combating 'the basic notion of human superiority we inherited from Renaissance humanism'. Here she introduced the idea of 'ecological humanism' that she upheld should replace 'humanism' per se. In an attempt to reverse the anthropogenic changes adversely affecting the environment, she advocated for a reciprocal relationship between humans and the natural world. Westling wrote:

[a]n ecological humanism would restore appropriate humility, absorbing the lessons of quantum physics and emphasizing cooperative participation within the

community of planetary life . . . Given such an understanding, we should develop a
sacramental awareness of the world, perhaps through the concept of an 'ecological
sublime' that accepts confirmation of its astonishment . . . instead of seeking or
presuming control [*sic*]. (1104)

The ameliorative task, similar to the one outlined by Westling that *Walden*
aims to accomplish is through:

1. Establishing and simultaneously questioning the attitudinal changes
   informing the nineteenth-century American society and by
   extension the human civilization under various stages of
   modernization.
2. Directing human gaze to the non-human world.
3. Pointing to the necessity for a harmonious relationship with Nature
   for holistic (human) development with an emphasis upon the need
   for intellectual growth.

Thoreau saw American capitalism as a force that would ultimately ravage
all wild nature on the continent, and later the world itself. In sympathy with
nature and blaming all 'civilized men' for the destruction of the natural world,
he felt it was his duty to raise his voice against the heedless exploitation of
nature. Born in Concord, Massachusetts, Henry David Thoreau, a reformist
at heart, was critical of the changes that had come to affect all aspects of
life for which he blamed the forces of industrialization and the consequent
transformation of the social set-up. A new generation was in the making,
a generation that perceived old ideas as redundant and desired freedom
from conventions. In *Journey Through Despair (1880–1914): Transformations
in British Literary Culture*, John A. Lester (Jr.) notes the twin contrasting
reactions to such change. If the eagerness and excitement for a new dawn
of socio-economic development had led to the spirit of living life to its
maximum, witnessed in the (self-reliance) of Ralph Waldo Emerson or the
encompassing, transcendentalist approach of Walt Whitman, it had also led
to illusion and despair. The realization that the century was coming to an
end also accentuated the mood of despair.

The response to the consequent feeling of pessimism emerged in
two forms: first, a direct opposition or gladness, and second, cynicism.
Humans either believed in the divine plan or responded as cynical self-
seekers, doubting all and becoming staunch followers of materialism. This
materialistic urge led to a renewed reliance on nature. Humans responded
to ('the magnificent enjoyment of the natural gods, the earth and sun and
fruits thereof . . . to be always in company with the sun, and sea, and earth',
and to find 'the faith that grows in the open air') (cited in Lester Jr. 1968:
73). The recourse to nature was more of a flight from the urban world than

seeking a haven in the welcoming faith that nature extended. Both Whitman and Thoreau were an inspiration for those who sought nature, as a means of reunion with the ancient ways of life and belief systems that bound humans with the natural world as well as their own system of beliefs. Chaos had given way to harmony, which was reflected in the spirit of oneness that pervaded the human and the non-human world. Richard Jeffries writes, '[We are] part and parcel of the great community of living beings, indissolubly connected with them from the lowest to the highest by a thousand ties' (cited in Lester Jr. 1968: 75).

Thoreau found contemporary civilization to be unsympathetic to its denizens, whereas nature exhibited an indescribable innocence and beneficence that goaded people towards finer feelings. He could not reiterate enough the constant need for urbanized humans to return to nature to fulfil their spiritual needs. Where the city landscape revealed only mountains of concrete and a cramped environment, the natural landscape unfurled a vista of beauty and uncluttered expanse. Totally enamoured by the beauty of the Walden Pond Thoreau wrote, 'A lake is a landscape's most beautiful and expressive feature. It is earth's eye; looking into which the beholder measures the depth of his own nature. The fluviatile trees next to the shore are the slender eyelashes which fringe it, and the wooded hills and cliffs around are its overhanging brows' (1986: 25). Commenting on the ecopoetics of Thoreau, Laura Dassow Walls says that he did not live in pristine wilderness but on the outskirts of Boston, 'on land that had been cut over, farmed, and abused for generations'. Walls applauds his ability to see beauty in this land and 'to make it stand, symbolically', for she believes that 'the principle of wild nature can help twenty-first-century generations to recover the desperately abused land they will inherit from us, and to see in it beauty, hope, regeneration' (Walls 2004: 5, 16).

Decades later D.H Lawrence would question: 'Why do modern people almost invariably ignore the things that are actually present to them ...' He believed that instead of inhabiting their physical space lived in abstractions and 'Talking to them' was 'like trying to have a human relationship with the letter X in Algebra' (as qtd. by Bantock 1983: 33–4).

Lawrence would also make pithy conclusions, 'It is our being cut off that is our ailment, and out of this ailment everything bad arises. I wish I saw a little clearer how you got over this cut-offness.... Myself, I suffer badly from being so cut off. But what is one to do?.... One has no real human relations—that is so devastating' (as qtd. By Holloway 1983: 98).

The remedy to Lawrence's diagnosis had already been proposed by Thoreau in the preceding century. It lay, according to him, in being simple, free, stable and flourishing as nature, and in correcting the attitude of being attached to and enamored by transitory objects. Philosopher par excellence,

Thoreau provided a simple solution to the metaphysical problems of modern civilization. He was convinced that by imposing upon nature and by excluding it from their lives, human beings were destroying their vitality, their health and happiness and above all the serenity and contentment that proximity to nature affords. Thoreau celebrates the healing properties of the clean, morning air:

What is the pill which will keep us well, serene and contented? Not my or thy great-grandfather's, but, our great grandmother Nature's universal vegetable, botanic medicines, by which she kept herself young always.... Morning air! If men will not drink of this at the fountainhead of the day, why, then, we must even bottle up some subscription ticket to morning time in this world. (1986: 93)

According to Thoreau, striving for luxuries was fruitless and unrewarding. He advocated a simple life, lived with the aid of bare necessities where people would be connected not only with their outer self but their inner being as well.

Resentful of the growing mechanization of the world, the symbol of which to him was the locomotive, he writes:

The whistle of the locomotive penetrates my woods summer and winter, sounding like the scream of a hawk sailing over a farmer's yard, informing that many restless city merchants are arriving within the circle of the town, or adventurous country traders from the other side.... With such huge and lumbering civility the country hands a chair to the city. All the Indian huckleberry hills are stripped off, all the cranberry meadows are raked into the city. Up comes the cotton, down goes the woven cloth; up comes the silk, down goes the woollen; up comes the books, but down goes the wit that writes them. (1986: 77–8)

Thoreau's resentment of the locomotive also stemmed from the fact that such an easy mode of transportation provided the inhabitants of the city a facile means for pillaging the forests for their material gains. With a note of acerbity he comments on the new replacing the old and the consequent fall in standards. He implores the valiant hero of an English ballad, Moore the dragon slayer to do away with this talisman of technological development, the locomotive. It was also seen by Thoreau as a symbol of capitalistic tendency which if unchecked, he felt, would maraud nature bare of its beauty. Emerson notes about Thoreau that he loved nature so well and was so happy in her solitude that he became very resentful and jealous of cities and the changes that they had brought about at the cost of the natural world that fell prey to human greed. 'Thank God', he said, 'they cannot cut down the clouds!' 'All kinds of figures are drawn on the blue ground with this fibrous white paint' (Thoreau as qtd. by Emerson 1986: 280).

Thoreau was dismayed with the modern farming system too as he saw it stripped of all its former rituals and religious significance, an indication of the irreverence that Nature was increasingly being subjected to through the course of time. He finds it disconcerting that modern people have no festivals or ceremonies to consecrate nature and even the farmer failed to acknowledge the sacredness of his calling. Thus, he concludes, that 'the landscape is deformed, husbandry degraded, and the farmer leads the meanest of lives'.

An astute observer, Thoreau blamed the attitudinal shift of people to blame for the insensitive treatment of nature. Once husbandry had been seen as a scared art as suggested by ancient poetry in mythology, he noted, only to be replaced by a remarkable apathy that ignoring the sacral aspect of nature with no festival, procession or ceremony to express gratitude for the unselfish bounties dispensed, except Thanksgiving 'regarding the soil as property, or the means of acquiring property chiefly' thus he reasons', the landscape is 'deformed, husbandry is degraded' and 'the farmer leads the meanest of lives'. He knows Nature but as a robber (1986: 111).

In *The Golden Bough*, James Frazer points towards the same idea of the myth of a dying and resurrected god underlying primitive fertility cults in different cultures and historical epochs. Frazer interprets the god to be a symbol of a vegetation deity, his death and resurrection represented in the annual cycle of seasons. Primitive people attributed the fluctuations of growth and decay, reproduction and dissolution, to the marriage, death and rebirth of gods. They also believed that by performing some of the religious rites and rituals they could aid the god who was the force of life in the struggle with the force of death. These rites that enacted the death, burial or drowning and the resurrection of god, tied people firmly to their lands and the surrounding environment.

In the same critical vein, Thoreau draws his readers' attention to 'cutting peat in a bog'. A bog is a wetland that accumulates acidic, fertile peat. Bogs are very sensitive habitats and are of great importance for biodiversity and 'cutting peat in a bog' is akin to scraping the pond of its very coat, Walden Pond here. Through various instances, Thoreau shows how humans have degenerated from their attitude of reciprocity towards the environment to one, which is characterized solely by exploitation:

In the winter of '46–7 there came a hundred men of Hyperborean extraction swoop down on to our pond one morning . . . They said that a gentleman farmer, who was behind the scenes, wanted to double his money, which, as I understood, amounted to half a million already; but in order to cover each one of his dollars with another, he took off the only coat, ay, the skin itself, of Walden Pond in the midst of a hard winter. They went to work at once, ploughing, harrowing, rolling, furrowing in admirable order as if they were bent on making this model farm; but when I was looking sharp to see what kind of seed they dropped into the furrow, a gang of fellows by my side suddenly began to hook up the virgin mould itself, with a peculiar jerk, clean down to the sand, or rather the water—for it was a very springy soil—indeed all the terra-firma there was—and haul it away on sleds, and then I guessed that they must be cutting peat in a bog. (1986: 194–5)[1]

It is with utter disappointment that Thoreau concludes: 'Nature has no human inhabitant who appreciates her. The birds with their plumage and their notes are in harmony with the flowers, but what youth or maiden conspires with the luxuriant beauty of Nature? She flourishes most alone, far from the towns where they reside. Talk of heaven! Ye disgrace earth' (1986: 134).

In 'Walden's "Political Thoreau"', Paul Friedrich also notes the discontentment registered in *Walden* against this weakening human-environmental tie and the exploitative attitude of humans towards nature. Friedrich writes that in telling sentences and paragraphs Thoreau makes his point against slash lumbering around his beloved pond and about the local farmers who acted as robbers of nature standing in contrast to the Roman farmers worshipping Ceres, the goddess of grain and harvests. The harvesting of ice by mechanical labourers is also seen as akin to the rape of the lake which she survives regenerating with the 'strength of her virginal purity' remaining intact (2008: 50).

In the chapter, 'Brute Neighbors', Thoreau directs the gaze of the reader beyond the non-human world by giving an account of all the beings inhabiting the wild, unseen to the unobservant eyes, clearly visible to him. He finds it remarkable how many creatures live freely though secretly in the woods, and still sustain themselves in the neighbourhood of towns, suspected by hunters only (1986: 151). For him, the world of nature and the wildlife therein have as much importance as of humans. Going a step further he asserts that he finds non-humans more humane than humans.

Thoreau directs the gaze of his readers to the animal world, that the otter grows to be four feet long, the size of a small boy; the raccoon, his neighbour, which stayed behind his house in the woods, whose voice, 'whinnering' at night he heard. The family of the woodcock, which gave him company while he had his lunch, all the while trying to attract his attention; the turtledoves, which sat over the stream Thoreau had dug and which fluttered from one bough to another of the soft white pines. Inquisitive red squirrels running down the same pines, and the ants, which enthralled him by their 'great' war.

He takes note of the hooting of the owl, the honking of the geese, the foxes with their demoniac barking, the red squirrel coursing over the roof and sides of the house, the rabbits that emerged at twilight and at night for their meal, the thieving jays picking up the kernels dropped by the squirrels, the chickadees, thriving on the crumbs the squirrels had dropped, thus making a case for their rightful space on the Earth through his writings.

Thoreau's most memorable statement on the value of wilderness occurs in the chapter, 'Spring' in *Walden*. By envisioning the unexplored forests and meadows as places where people can become rejuvenated and revitalized by the presence of the wild, he makes a case for the protection and conservation of the natural world. He writes that the village life would stagnate had it not been for wilderness, the 'unexplored forests and meadows' surrounding it; the necessity of the 'tonic of wildness' for the 'mysterious and un-explorable' land and sea that remains uncharted due to its unfathomable nature, a force that reminds of human diminutiveness against the natural world, exhilarating and challenging by its very nature (1986: 209-10).

Where the city landscape reveals only mountains of concrete the rural landscape embedded in the lap of nature unfurls a vista of beauty that thrills the eyes and calms the heart. In its multi-pronged approach toward the non-human and the human, *Walden* becomes a treatise that subscribes to ecological humanism—the humility that humans should have towards the non-human world for a more harmonious relationship between the two. Responding to the challenges in the path of the inculcation of such a spirit of harmony, Wendell Berry says, 'One way to answer this challenge is to sink one's roots more deeply in place, it is only in the place one belongs to, intimate and familiar, long watched over that the hawk stoops into the clearing before one's eyes; the wood drake alone and serene in his glorious plumage, swims out of his hiding place' (cited in James McKusick 2000: 167).

The scene in *Walden* describing the boat ride is reminiscent of William Wordsworth's adventure in the *Prelude* where the young poet stole out one night to enjoy boating. The difference however is that Thoreau experiences the same fun without the guilt of having acquired a stolen boat. Both the litterateurs practised and advocated their celebrated spirit of harmony with nature. However, the note of lament recurs when Thoreau expresses the sense of anguish at the depletion of the environment running through his work while speaking of woodchoppers plundering the forests. Making a touching plea on behalf of nature he asks, 'How can you expect the birds to sing when their groves are cut down?' Lawrence Buell comments, 'the path to biocentrism must lead through humanitarianism. Human denizens of the modernized world are most likely to move toward ecocentric ways of thinking when the sympathetic bond is activated. . . . But to activate that altruism . . . some projection of empathy from self to the other is necessary' (1996: 386–7).

The hounding of the fox in the Walden woods is symbolic of the way humans take over land hounding other living beings out of their homes, robbing them of their rightful space. Thoreau recollects hearing sometimes in the dark winter mornings and in winter afternoons a pack of hounds chasing through the woods with wild noises, along with the note of the hunting horn at intervals.

The river's living creatures also elicit a deep sympathy from Thoreau. He affectionately describes how he befriended the sunfish.[2] As he and the fish are tied in the bond of innocent trust, so in *Walden* the woodcock and her brood share a bond with him. Commenting on the devastation of the Shad fishery that resulted from the construction of the Billerica Dam, Thoreau observes that shads are still taken in the basin of the Concord River at Lowell and empathizes with them, voicing protest against the non-human world in touching terms, 'When Nature gave thee instinct, gave she thee the heart to bear thy fate?.... I for one am with thee, and who knows what may avail a crow-bar against that Billerica dam?.... Who hears the fishes when they cry?' (cited in McKusick 2000: 146). This outpouring of solicitude here anticipates the equally woeful and prophetic words of Pia, one of the central characters in the postcolonial writer Amitav Ghosh's *The Hungry Tide*, while reflecting upon environmental ethics and justice, at a time when the destruction of the natural world has increased manifolds. The twenty-first century Pia defending the rights of the non-humans argues with another character Kanai, furthering the cause of the non-humans, as highlighted by Thoreau, questioning the anthropocentric attitude, 'Just suppose we cross that imaginary line that prevents us from deciding that no other species matters except ourselves. What'll be left then? Aren't we alone enough in the universe?'('The Hungry Tide', 301).

In *The Maine Woods*, Thoreau calls for the establishment of national preserves for providing sanctuary to the, now universally threatened, non-humans. His keen sense of identity between humans and non-humans is explicitly affirmed in his advocacy for the protection of the pine trees from the commercial lumbering enterprises that threaten their destruction:

Strange that so few ever come to the woods to see how the pine lives and grows and spires, lifting its evergreen arms to the light—to see its perfect success; but most are content to behold it in the shape of many broad boards brought to market, and deem that its true success! But the pine is no more lumber than man is, and to be made into board and houses is no more its true and highest use than the truest use of a man is to be cut down and made into manure. There is a higher law affecting our relation to pines as well as to men. A pine cut down, a dead pine is no more a pine than a dead human carcass is a man. (cited in McKusick 2000: 167)

Christopher Hitt observes in his essay, 'Toward an Ecological Sublime' that environmental philosophy teaches it is estrangement from nature which is the problem of the current environmental situation. In this context it becomes important to endorse concepts that foster harmony with nature so as to overcome the binary opposition between the two entities of man and nature. And once the realization dawns that we are 'literal participants' in the scheme of things, 'then we will realize that to harm nature is to harm ourselves. Nature, is then, an extended self, and is entitled to the same concern as any other person' (1999: 612).

What James Lovelock would expound later as the Gaia hypothesis, Thoreau had already comprehended much earlier. Thus, he speaks of the earth not as a dead object but as a single, living entity, functioning as a unitary organism. Observing the phenomena of thawing clay and sand is a delightful experience for him. The forms, which the thawing sand and clay assume in flowing down the sides of a deep cut on the railroad through which he passed on his way to the village capture his attention. In this material, Thoreau reads the beginning of creation and what can be interpreted as the initiation of the human mind into the sphere of enlightenment bringing about the erasure of the binaries, human and nature by lightening the commonality between the two:

I feel as if I were nearer to the vitals of the globe, for this sandy overflow is something such a foliaceous mass as the vitals of the animal body. You find thus in the very sands an anticipation of the vegetable leaf. No wonder that the earth expresses itself outwardly in leaves, it so labors with the idea inwardly. . . . Thus, also, you pass from the lumpish grub in the earth to the airy and fluttering butterfly. The very globe continually transcends and translates itself, and becomes winged in its orbit. (1986: 203)

Thoreau extolled the simplicity in the life of the savage man and hoped, therefore, that the civilized man would always remain a savage at heart, though a wiser and a more experienced one. Lamenting the fallout of civilization on contemporary men and women he felt that their manners had been corrupted, their religions had failed to redeem them, and there was a sense of spiritual desolation that permeated their lives. They no longer lived life according to the dictates of native wisdom based on independence and magnanimity. According to Thoreau, living in this manner required the attainment of true knowledge of the self and people can know themselves best, he felt, only if they know and fully understand their natural environment. His observations and propositions in this regard are equally pertinent even today.

Comparing the savage state of society with modern civilized life, Thoreau concludes that in primitive times people worked hard, and were happier. Karl Marx's hypothesis on the pervading feeling of alienation in modern society bolsters the idea that humans are by essence creators but in concrete, historical contexts, their creative urge is crushed. Marx captures poignantly the plight of the human, 'in his work, therefore, he does not affirm himself but denies himself, does not feel content but unhappy, does not develop freely his physical and mental energy but mortifies his body and ruins his mind ... the external character of labour for the worker appears in the fact that it is not his own, but someone else's, that it does not belong to him, that in it he belongs, not to himself, but to another' (1974: 129). An attempt to address this condition is extended by Timothy Clark in 'Phenomenology', where he argues that human relation to things around is essentially intentional (i.e. in the sense of necessarily relating to something outside the self). For any such intentionality to prevail, it is to be assumed that the world is a 'totality of such relations', for, if there exists any dualism leading to a schism between the isolated consciousness and the realm of objects on the other, it shall only lead to confusion, 'falsely dividing an existence which was already, fundamentally and originality, a "being-in-the-world"' (2014: 277–8).

Adding to his observation of the imbalance in the distribution of wealth under the capitalist system and the resultant sense of social dissatisfaction, Thoreau says that the problem may have different facets but its root cause can be traced to human alienation with the non-human world and the thoughtless herd mentality of modern society.

When Thoreau speaks of the farmer in *Walden*, he speaks in favour of the expression of human's creative potential. 'Who knows', he had asked, 'but if men constructed their dwellings with their own hands, and provided food for themselves and families simply and honestly enough, the poetic faculty would be universally developed, as birds universally sing when they are so engaged?' (1986: 31) Martin Heidegger shared a similar opinion when in 'Building Dwelling Thinking' (1951) he discussed the art of dwelling. Heidegger believed dwelling is to create and caringly maintain a place of habitation within 'the fourfold' comprising the earth/land with its particular topography, waterways, and biotic community; sky, including the alternation of night and day, the rhythm of the seasons, and the vagaries of the weather; divinities, those emissaries or traces that yet remain of an absent god; and fellow humans. This involved attuning oneself in that which one thinks, does, and makes to that which is given with earth and sky: that is, a particular natural environment. It implied also leaving open a space for the incalculable possibility of divine visitation, while acknowledging one's own mortality and the ties that bind one to fellow mortals, as well as to the place in which one dwells. *Above all*, writes Heidegger, 'Mortals dwell insofar as they save the earth', whereby, 'to save' (*retten*) is to be understood not so much in the sense of 'rescue', but rather of freeing something into 'its own presencing' (*etwas in sein eigenes Wesen freilassen*) meaning allowed to exist in its free state (Rigby 2004: 430–1), as Thoreau did.

Japanese scholar Shoko Itoh draws an interesting parallel between the two authors Thoreau and the Japanese writer and ascetic Kamo no Chomei's *Hojoki* (1212) (translated and published in 1905 as *Japanese Thoreau of Twelfth*

Century). Like Thoreau, Chomei also led a secluded life out of choice; however, Chomei's seclusion was longer. He secluded himself from public life when he was fifty and lived in a hermitage called Hojo until his death at age sixty-three. Both Thoreau's cabin and Chomei's Hojo are small, simple dwellings created by their dwellers, their lives of austerity leading them to spirituality and their ability to create music (Thoreau played the flute and Chomei the four stringed Japanese lute) uniting them with their surroundings, a 'searching for spiritual salvation by forming a soundscape full of natural sound in harmony with flute and lute respectively' (2004–5: 36).

The simple and homely task of hoeing of beans attaching Thoreau deeply to the earth and he feels a satisfaction hitherto unknown. Ecstatic, he exclaims, 'I came to love my rows, my beans, though so many more than I wanted. They attached me to the earth, and so I got strength like Antaeus ...' (1986: 103–4).

In Walden Thoreau was home. For the discerning reader *Walden*, thus, becomes a manifesto for ecological humanism and a strong plea for environmental justice; Thoreau not only critiques the materialistic, exploitative approach of society towards nature he also proposes remedial measures for undoing the wrongs done to the environment. He advocates a way of life in sync with the world of nature and thereby, a more balanced way of existence given largely to intellectual pursuits. Thoreau's ecopoetics is thus in favour of physical nature and for restoring its rightful place in the world.

Notes

1. Thoreau was shocked by the crowd of men who descended on the Walden Pond in the winter of 1846–7. These men were sent by a rich farmer to make his lands more fertile by scraping away the fertile soil of the pond for layering his land with it. A dejected Thoreau notes, '... a gang of fellows by my side suddenly began to hook up the virgin mould itself ... and haul it away on sleds, and then I guessed that they must be cutting peat in a bog' (1986: 194–5).
2. Thoreau writes that he had befriended the sunfish by standing much time with them, stroking them familiarly 'suffering them to nibble his fingers harmlessly' (cited in McKusick 2000: 146).

References

Bakratcheva, Albena, Casado da Rocha, Antonio Itoh, Shoko et al., 'Thoreau's "Walden" in the Global Community', *I*, n.s., vols. 12–13, 2004–5, pp. 18–58.

Bantock, G.H., 'The Social and Intellectual Background', *The New Pelican Guide to English literature, vol. 7: From James to Eliot*, ed. Boris Ford, London and USA: Penguin Books, 1983.

Buell, Lawrence, *The Environmental Imagination: Thoreau, Nature Writing, and the Formation of American Culture*, London: The Belknap Press of Harvard University Press, 1996.

Clark, Timothy, 'Phenomenology', in *The Oxford Handbook of Ecocriticism,* ed. Greg Garrard, USA: Oxford University Press, 2014.

Coombs, Amy, *Frontiers in Ecology and the Environment*, vol. 12, no. 4, May 2014, p. 208

Friedrich, Paul, 'Walden's "Political Thoreau"', *The Concord Saunterer*, n.s., vol. 16, 2008, pp. 45–58, The Thoreau Society, Inc, <http://www.jstor.org/stable/23395086>, accessed on 27 July 2015.

Ghosh, Amitav, *The Hungry Tide*, London: Harper Collins, 2005.

Hitt, Christopher, 'Toward an Ecological Sublime', *New Literary History*, vol. 30, no. 3, Summer 1999, Virginia: John Hopkins University Press, 1999.

Holloway, John, 'The Literary Scene', *The New Pelican Guide to English Literature, Vol. 7: From James to Eliot*, ed. Boris Ford, London and USA: Penguin Books, 1983.

Kueffer Christoph and Christopher N. Kaiser-Bunbury, 'Reconciling conflicting perspectives for biodiversity conservation in the Anthropocene', *Frontiers in Ecology and the Environment*, vol. 12, no. 2, March 2014, pp. 131–7.

Lester (Jr.) John A., *Journey Through Despair (1880–1914): Transformations in British Literary Culture*, New Jersey: Princeton University Press, 1968.

Marx, K., *Economic and Philosophic Manuscripts of 1844*, Moscow: Moscow Publishers, 1974.

McKusick, James, 'Henry David Thoreau: Life in the Woods', *Green Writing: Romanticism and Ecology*, London: MacMillan, 2000.

Palsson Gisli, 'Human: Environmental Relations: Orientalism, Paternalism and Communalism', *Nature and Society: Anthropological Perspectives*, ed. Phillipe Descola and Gisli Palsson, London: Routledge, 1996, pp. 63–79.

Symons, Arthur, *Harper's New Monthly Magazine*, vol. LXXXVII, November 1893.

Rigby, Kate, 'On the (Im)possibility of Ecopoiesis', *New Literary History*, vol. 35, no. 3, *Critical Inquiries, Explorations, and Explanations*, Summer 2004, pp. 427–42.

Thoreau, Henry, *Walden And Civil Disobedience*, ed. Owen Thomas, New Delhi: Prentice Hall of India, 1986.

Wagler, Ron, 'The Anthropocene Mass Extinction: An Emerging Curriculum Theme for Science Educators', *The American Biology Teacher*, vol. 73, no. 2, February 2011, pp. 78–83.

Walls, Laura Dassow, 'Thoreau's "Walden" in the Twenty-first Century', *The Concord Saunterer*, n.s., vols. 12–13, 2004–5, pp. 6–17.

Westling, Louise, 'Forum on Literatures of Environment', *PMLA*, vol. 114, 1999, p. 1089.

7

Environmental Praxis through Literature

RASHMI LEE GEORGE

THE NATIVE AMERICAN INDIANS have traditionally protected and nurtured the lands that they had lived in for thousands of years. For them the connection between humans and land has always been sacrosanct. However, for the colonizers land was an object to be possessed, property to be owned. The colonizers brought with them the hierarchical demarcation between land and people. In the second half of the twentieth century, the Native Americans became witness to several layers of environmental exploitation and pollution. 'Water tainted with industrial waste, strip mining, radiation exposure causing illness or even death, toxic groundwater killing livestock or crops, and native lands targeted for waste dumps and landfills are just a few of the problems Native peoples faced in their homelands' (Dreese 2002: 89). The environmental injustice meted out to the Native Americans in the form of environmental racism is one of the major concerns against which writers such as Simon Ortiz have written about. This essay explores select poems of Simon Ortiz in order to study his response to environmental racism and its consequences not only on Native Americans but on other communities too. His writings against environmental injustice and racism could be considered his praxis against the forces of colonization.

The term environmental racism entered into political discourse in 1987 when the United Church of Christ's Commission for Racial Justice (UCC-CRJ) published a report that found race to be the leading factor in the choice of location of commercial hazardous waste facilities. The UCC-CRJ report determined that people of colour suffered a 'disproportionate risk' to the health of their families and their environments: 60 per cent of African Americans and Latinos, and more than 50 per cent of Asian/Pacific Islanders and Native Americans were living in areas with one or more uncontrolled toxic waste disposal sites. In the report, Reverend Benjamin Chavis, then executive director of the UCC's commission on Racial Justice, defined environmental racism as 'racial discrimination in environmental policymaking and the enforcement of regulations and laws, the deliberate targeting of people of colour communities of toxic waste facilities, the official sanctioning of the life threatening presence of poisons and pollutants in our communities, and history of excluding people of colour from leadership in the environmental movements' (Chavis 1998: 304).

Although the term environmental racism might have been relatively new in 1982, according to Kamala Platt, the practice of environmental racism was certainly not. In the article 'Ecocritical Chicana Literature' she writes, 'The beginnings of environmental racism can be dated to the onset of European colonization and later when American Indian tribes who once inhabited life-sustaining environments were removed to landscapes far less fertile or lacking the natural resources necessary for survival' (ISLE Summer 1996: 69). In some cases, the lands of the Native American Indians were snatched away. Often measures, such as open-pit mining, re-routing of rivers, etc., were adopted for commercial purposes regardless of the adverse fallout on the Native American communities who lived in close proximity to such activities. Many prolific American Indian writers have written about the (dense) relationship between humans and the land. In fact, it has become almost a cliché in Native American Studies to observe that contemporary American Indian writers study the relationship between humans and the land, but novels such as *Ceremony* and *Almanac of the Dead* by Leslie Marmon Silko are not set in the sublime wilderness, spaces exalted by many mainstream American environmentalists and nature writers. Instead, they are 'set on reservations, in open-pit uranium mines, and in national and international borderlands. These novels question and confront our most popular assumptions about "nature" and "nature writing" by drawing attention to the contested terrains where increasing numbers of poor and marginalized people are organizing around interrelated social and environmental problems' (Adamson 2001: xvii). Simon Ortiz likewise locates his poetry in a hazardous zone.

In case of Native American literature, stories and myths from oral traditions infuse American Indian voices, combining history with the present to create rich and often complex literatures. The complexity is seen in the sense that boundaries are blurred between the past and the present, between history and myth, and between the physical and the spiritual. It is often a literature of impassioned anger and unequivocal resistance as American Indian writers strive to speak for themselves and claim authority over their histories. This activism/praxis asserts itself differently in each writer and creates a literature that attempts to heal and decolonize fragmented and disappearing cultures. The stories connect the people to their land, history and cultural identity. Lee Schweninger states that 'the earth, the word, the speaker of the word, and the story are inseparable. They exist within the same lines of dependence as the biosphere' (Schweninger 1993: 57). In fact, the Gaia theory recognizes the earth as a living and conscious organism. When British atmospheric scientist, James Lovelock propounded his Gaia hypothesis in the early 1980s, it shocked the scientific world that the earth could be viewed on such a global scale, as a single living entity, whose constituents function in order to maintain equilibrium or homeostasis. The theory was received favourably by indigenous commentators because the hypothesis was not new to them. Contemporary Laguna writer Paula Gunn Allen clarifies the notion prevalent among American Indian communities of the earth as a living being: 'An Indian, at the deepest level of being, assumes that the earth is alive in the same sense that human beings are alive. This aliveness is seen in nonphysical terms, in terms that are perhaps familiar to the mystic or the psychic, and this view gives rise to a metaphysical sense of reality that is an ineradicable part of Indian awareness' (Allen 1986: 70). The Gaia theory thus re-affirmed the age-old practice of revering the environment prevalent among the indigenous cultures. It also introduced an ethical consciousness into environmental studies of the Western world.

Similarly, Gary Snyder, known as the poet laureate of deep ecology, a very prominent form of environmentalism, suggests that deep ecology demands recognition of the intrinsic value of nature. Greg Garrard says, 'It identifies the dualistic separation of humans from nature promoted by Western philosophy and culture as the origin of environmental crisis and demands a return to a monistic, primal identification of humans and the ecosphere' (Garrard 2004: 21). The shift from a human-centred to a nature-centred system of values is the core of the radicalism attributed to deep ecology, thus pitting it against the whole gamut of Western philosophy and religion. Therefore, ecocriticism like some American Indian philosophies promotes and teaches the interdependence and connectedness of all living things, which means that any study of human existence, would be incomplete if it did not place human beings within an ecological context. Most Native American Indian cultures have evolved from the legacy of a tradition that cares for the landscape with reverence and reciprocity. That which is procured from the land is returned through prayer and ceremony to maintain the balance upon which all life rests. In Donnelle Dreese's words, 'Deep ecology sees the scope of all environmental exploitation as symptomatic of a much deeper nature/human relational breakdown' (Dreese 2002: 6). It seeks to enquire into more profound questions that concern human interaction with the natural world rather than the 'shallow' issues such as pollution or extinction of species which it recognizes as symptoms rather than the cause of environmental degradation. 'Deep ecology is concerned with encouraging an egalitarian attitude on the part of humans not only towards all members of the ecosphere, but even towards all identifiable entities or forms in the ecosphere. This attitude is intended to extend for example to such entities (or forms) as rivers, landscapes and even species and social systems considered in their own right' (Fox 1995: 269–70).

Many Native American writings reflect the oneness of human beings with their land and the consequent linkage to their history, tribal myths, traditions and customs. Therefore, writers from the Native American community delve into their traditions, myths, history and the connection with the land while writing their stories. The very essence of their lives, thus, gets transferred into their stories. Suzanne Lundquist opines, 'Contemporary Native American authors have turned to creative non-fiction or literary autoethnography to express how tribal affiliations, myths, ancestry, gender, life stages, education, geographical, local, and historical moments impress their consciousness and inform their identity and works' (Lundquist 2004: 8). These authors also see themselves 'in relation to collective social units or groups' rather than as isolated individuals (Krupat 1992: 8). Brian Swann says that contemporary American Indian poets seem to work from a sense of social responsibility to the group as much as from an intense individuality. Their poetry, therefore, according to Brian Swann, 'is the poetry of historic witness' (Swann 1988: xvii). He further adds, 'The Native American poet is his or her history with all its ambiguities and complications' (Swann 1988: xviii). Lastly, Swann sees in Native American poetry: 'a desire for wholeness—for balance, reconciliation, and healing—within the individual, the tribe, the community, the nation; one sees an insistence on these things, on growth, on rich survival' (Swann 1988: xxxi).

Bearing testimony to this outlook of the Native American poet is Simon Ortiz's *Fight Back: For the Sake of the People, For the Sake of the Land* (1980), a mixed collection of poetry and prose that draws connections between the twentieth-century struggles of American Indian people, their fight to protect their communities and resources and the Pueblo Revolt of 1680. In 1992, Ortiz published *Woven Stone*, a collection of previously published volumes of poetry—*Going for Rain* (1976), *A Good Journey* (1977) and *Fight Back: For the Sake of the People, For the Sake of the Land* (1980). This third volume most fully voices the ecological problems that have become inescapable for American Indian people facing environmental ruin not of their own making. It is his most politicized work, following an oral narrative style, and is autobiographical and historical too in that it describes the destructive effects of the uranium industry of the 1960s on the people and the land of the Acoma Pueblo community where Ortiz grew up. *Fight Back: For the Sake of the People, For the Sake of the Land* is located near Deetseyamah (known as McCarthy's in the US and New Mexico maps), the Acoma farming village where Ortiz grew up in the 1940s and 1950s. It was a place abundant in water supply but during the 1880s the place experienced long periods of drought. With the construction of the railroad, a logging town and the Bluewater Dam in the 1930s, the place had very little water for farming. Therefore, the natives of the place took up jobs in rail road construction and in the Uranium and coal mines flourishing throughout the region. Simon Ortiz writes movingly about the Four Corners too in *Fight Back: For the Sake of the People, For the Sake of the Land*. He points out that by 1972, the region had become so toxically contaminated by the military testing of nuclear bombs and the mining of Uranium and coal that the Nixon administration sought to have it designated a National Sacrifice Area. Ortiz and many other writers like him directly and forcefully address environmental injustices. It is not only a form of action to create awareness of historical and present-day injustices but also a method to prevent future catastrophic possibilities.

Ortiz chronicles the various injustice shared by the American Indian community in north-west New Mexico. 'His poetry attempts to reproach the blind advancement of modern materialism and technology, expose American governmental hypocrisy, and urge action against environmental and social injustices' (Dreese 2002: 91). Ortiz had worked in the uranium mines and mills, which gave him many of the experiences he recounts in *Fight Back* and helped to form his social and political consciousness. In the poem titled, 'It was that Indian', Ortiz tells the story of a Navajo man named Martinez who found a green stone near his hogan and in the process discovered uranium along what is now the Grants mineral belt. He was celebrated, photographed 'in Kodak color' (Ortiz 1992: 295) and praised by 'the Chamber of Commerce' (Ortiz 1992: 295) as the Indian who brought prosperity to Grants. However, due to the enormous industrial expansion of the mines and mills, people complained about chemicals poisoning streams, mine cave ins, and cancer caused by uranium radiation. Consequently, Martinez was then blamed by the same Chamber of Commerce for the harmful side effects of the industry because he had discovered the piece of uranium. Used as a scapegoat by the government, Martinez came to be seen as the perpetrator of all the grave consequences of the government's use of uranium.

When the Native American Indians took jobs at the mines, they were mostly employed in inferior, hazardous positions because they had no mining experience. In the poem, 'Starting at the Bottom', their plight is captured in lines, such as 'The truth is,/ the companies didn't much care/ nor did the unions,/ even if both of them/ were working our land' (Ortiz 1992: 297). Dreese says, 'encountering severe racism, without education or social programmes for support, Native American Indians at the bottom of the hiring hierarchy would stay there, making minimal money' (Dreese 2002:

92). 'So, almost thirty years later,/ the Acoma men / were at the bottom/ of the underground mines at Ambrosia Lake,/ and the Laguna men/were at the bottom of the open pit at Jackpile,/ they were still training, gaining experience,/ and working their way up' (Ortiz 1992: 298). The Natives who remained in such low-ranking jobs were there not only because advanced positions were reserved for whites but also because these jobs were dangerous and the established racist attitude was that Natives were dispensable. The greatest advantage in employing the native American Indians in perilous jobs was that their deaths could easily be explained and accounted for by directing the responsibility for the death onto the Indian. No one challenged the negligence or neglect of an Indian. It was expected. The death of a white man on duty was something the industry had to clarify. 'Ray's Story' is a poem about a Muskogee Indian named Lacey who had the hazardous job of pulling from the ore pieces of dynamite, steel, and cable as it came down a chute into the primary crusher. Lacey was ordered not to turn off the crusher because it would slow down production. He became entangled in a cable, which pulled him through the crusher, and was instantly killed. The foreman, angered that the conveyor belt had stopped running, assumed Lacey was asleep and went to the pit. Seeing Lacey crushed up in the machine, he only said, 'Gawd, that Indian was big' (Woven Stone 1992: 303). Lacey was ultimately blamed for failing to turn off the crusher before removing the cable.

The Native American society disintegrated with colonization. Having depended on the land for food and shelter, Native cultures underwent dramatic changes due to European economic encroachment and governmental usurpation of Native lands for various uses such as laying railroad. Native ways of life and land-based survival methods clashed with government laws and ideas of civilization and development, which is why it became necessary for native Americans to work in the mines. In 'Final Solution: Jobs, Leaving' Ortiz tells how families were torn asunder because fathers had to migrate for employment. 'Goodbye. Goodbye Daddy. Daddy,/ please come back. Please don't go./ Daddy. But they would leave' (Ortiz 1992: 318). Through the typography of the poem itself, Ortiz conveys the disintegration in the family. 'We had to buy groceries,/ had to have clothes, homes, roofs,/ windows. Surrounded by the United States,/ we had come to need money./ The solution was to change,/ to leave, to go to jobs/' (Ortiz 1992: 318). Compelled to participate in the Western cultural economy, families were broken up and experienced new hardships that they could not counter.' 'In suffering literal physical removals, either onto reservations or to find work, the native communities who were devoted to and intrinsically connected to place underwent widespread cultural disintegration' (Dreese 2002: 93).

Throughout *Fight Back* Ortiz articulates his fervent ecological concerns and portrays the impact of industrial and technological advances on his homeland and the Native people who inhabited the land. In an interview with Kathleen Manley and Paul W. Rea, Ortiz states that to native cultures the 'land is a material reality as well as a philosophical, metaphysical idea or concept; land is who we are, land is our identity, land is home place, land is sacred' (Manley & Rea 1989: 365). This Native concept of land or place as identity expresses the belief that nature is connected with human life and it is this sense of place that defines a person's life. 'Understanding the bond between identity and the land is crucial to understanding nature's significance to Native cultures' (Dreese 2002: 93). However, in *Woven Stone*, Ortiz presents European ethnocentrism that justified exploitation of the land and betrayal of the Acoma people. When the first Spaniard entered the lands in 1540, 'he recommended occupation and settlement because of the natural material wealth of the land ... the land and the people were obviously productive and the potential for colonization and profit was worthy of royal and private investment' (Ortiz: 341, 342). Being concerned only with the monetary possibilities, the Spanish claimed the land as their own with no regard or concern for the people who inhabited those lands. Their obsession with intense development left the once lush and grassy area barren and arid. Ortiz writes, 'The railroads were the first large Industrial users of the water belonging to the land and people. They found it easy enough to get it; they simply took it' (Ortiz 1992: 343).

Ortiz lambasts land exploitation in *A Good Journey* with the poem 'A Designated National Park'. In the poem, Ortiz reproduces a notice found outside Montezuma Castle, Arizona, that announces the imposition of a fee in order to enter the place:

DESIGNATED FEDERAL RECREATION FEE AREA/ENTREE FEES/$1.00 FOR 1 DAY PERMIT/MONTEZUMA CASTLE ONLY INCLUDES PURCHASER/OR OTHERS WITH HIM IN PRIVATE NON-COMMERCIAL VEHICLE/$0.50 FOR 1 DAY PERMIT/MONTEZUMA CASTLE ONLY INCLUDES PURCHASER/ IN COMMERCIAL VEHICLE/AUTHORIZED/BY THE LAND AND WATER CONSERVATION FUND/ACT OF 1965.' (Ortiz 1992: 235)

In order to enter his home Ortiz would have had to buy a permit. He criticizes the Western practice of grabbing land by constructing artificial boundaries in order to claim ownership for the purpose of commercialization. According to William Cronon, 'more than anything else, it was the treatment of land and property as commodities traded at market that distinguished English conceptions of ownership from Indian ones' (Cronon 1983: 75). The tribes had a sense of belonging to a place rather than a sense of ownership. For them occupation of a certain territory did not mean ownership of that territory. The landscape with its spiritual significance was regarded a living entity beyond the jurisdiction of human claim or monetary value. The inability of the Native American Indians in reading or communicating in English contributed further to the robbery of their lands. The Natives could not live on their own terms after colonization commenced. Forced to follow foreign ways that were opposed to their cultural beliefs, the Acomas were susceptible to European domination and betrayal.

Ortiz exposes the ruthlessly capitalist spirit behind the so-called American Dream. Ortiz succinctly describes the black irony of American development in terms of its social and economic hypocrisy: 'The nation swept on into the twentieth century and the Mericano was not called thief or killer; instead he was a missionary, merchant and businessman, philanthropist, educator, civil servant, and worker' (Ortiz 1980: 350). Individuals practising the capitalist American Dream, or Manifest Destiny, were regarded as heroes or people making government to maintain control over the Native American Indians by, for example, using relatively unpopulated Indian lands for nuclear test site. While expounding on the demerits of American capitalism, Ortiz's activism/praxis expands the scope of victimization to include even people from Western cultural backgrounds affected by the cut-throat market forces of colonization. Near the end of 'Our Homeland, a National Sacrifice Area', Ortiz voices the danger that awaits 'all Americans' if their lives kept racing destructively in the same direction: 'If the survival and quality of the life of the Indian people is not assured, then no one else's life is, because those same economic, social, and political forces, which destroy them will surely destroy others' (Ortiz 1992: 360). Ortiz diminishes the gap between indigenous cultures and Western cultures by stressing on the place inhabited by all humans and the destructive forces to which all are vulnerable. Thus he addresses a multi-cultural space which is adversely affected by environmental degradation due to market forces of colonization.

Ortiz's *Fight Back: For the Sake of the People, For the Sake of the Land* is an example of his all-embracing spirit while discussing nature and culture. While portraying the plight of the Acoma people, he also highlights the sufferings of the poor white people. Further, he dwells on the unity and friendship which get created in the workplaces due to various kinds of suppression and marginalization faced by the Native American community and the economically backward (other) communities at the hands of the multinational corporations. His understanding of human relationship to nature developed in his family's fields and in a Kerr-MacGee Uranium mine, the locations where he observed the subjugation of his people and the annihilation of their lands. It is the experiences in these locations that gave him the impetus to write about the underlying reasons for the destruction of his people's lands. 'In both his poems and prose, he argues that the corporate colonization of the Four Corners region is nothing less than history repeating itself, this time in relation to who suffers the consequences of modern-day environmental pollution' (Adamson 2001: 62). While writing about the situation of the Acoma people, he is reminded about the Pueblo rebellion of 1680, which was against theft of land and resources, slave labour, religious persecution and demands for unjust tributes. And 300 years later similar conditions were being witnessed because of the activities of multinational corporations. In 'To Change in a Good Way', one of the poems based on his experience of working in the uranium industry, Ortiz poignantly illustrates that what is at stake is not only the survival of the Aacqumeh hanoh (the Acoma Pueblo people as they are called in their own language) or the Dine or other south-western American Indian people, but the survival of all the people of the nation. Ortiz recognizes that the Kerr-McGee was created to benefit the rich. Its managers were apathetic to the situation of the people and the land. 'Low wages and unsafe working conditions led to friendships at Kerr-McGee that might not have occurred outside the workplace in the racially tense climate of the United States in 1950s' (Adamson 2001: 63).

The poem 'To Change in Good Way' explores the friendship between an Oklahoma white couple Bill and Ida and a Laguna Pueblo couple Pete and Mary. Bill migrates along with his wife to work at Kerr-McGee's Ambrosia Lake Uranium mine in New Mexico. They live in a small trailer home. While carpooling to Section 17, Bill becomes friends with Pete who spends his after-work hours raising sheep and cultivating the same small plot of land where his Laguna ancestors had raised chili, sweet corn, squash and beans. Even after working for twenty years in the New Mexico mine, Bill longs to return to Oklahoma with enough resources to buy a piece of land. 'You're lucky you got some land, Pete/Bill would say./ It's not much but it's some land,/ Pete would agree' (Ortiz 1992: 309). Meanwhile, the wives become friends too. Mary gets an opportunity to see Ida's garden upon a visit to her trailer home. No vegetation grows in Ida's garden. The state of her garden is symbolic of how rootless the couple feel after migration. The New Mexican soil's refusal to produce any yield for Bill and Ida also represents their emptiness and barrenness in the new place. When Mary sees the wilted lettuce and radishes, and the corn that failed to thrive in Ida's garden, she suggests that her soil needs 'something in it' that she needs to break up with the heavy, packed clay. She promises to come back the next weekend with some sheep dung to knead into the soil. 'Ida's garden suggests one of the most recurrent themes of *Fight Back*—to survive, humans must recognize a reciprocal relationship with the land' (Adamson 2001: 64). By nourishing and softening the hard red clay with sheep dung, Ida establishes a reciprocal relationship with the land, putting her time and care into the ground so that it will become more sustainably productive. She also manifests that all uses of land are not destructive. Additionally, Pete and Mary's warm and friendly intervention in the lives of Bill and Ida enable the latter to cope with their grief when Bill's brother Slick gets killed in Vietnam.

Ortiz exalts many Native American customs and traditions which promise peace, healing and restoration. He not only presents their benefits for the natives but also stresses on the beneficial impact they have on people from other culture. When Bill's beloved younger brother, Slick, is killed by stepping on a US landmine on his second tour on duty in Vietnam, Pete and Mary arrive at Bill's trailer, bearing feathered prayer sticks and some Indian corn they have cultivated in their garden. Pete tells Bill to plant the corn, a symbol of the sacred relationship between humans and the earth, as a reminder that Slick will now be given back to earth to grow like a seed. 'Just like Slick will be planted again/He'll be like that, like seed planted,/like corn seed, the Indian corn' (Ortiz 1992: 313). Ortiz writes, Corn cannot 'be regarded as anything less than a sacred and holy and respected product of the creative forces of life, land, and the people's responsibilities and relationships to each other and to the land' (Ortiz 1992: 346). Pete instructs Bill to put the prayer sticks, which symbolize Slick's journey from this life to another place of being, somewhere, he thinks Slick might be able to help change life in a good way. Pete's gifts and his instructions on how to use them give Bill an insight into the economic, social, and political connections between his work for low wages in dangerous mine shafts and Slick's death in a jungle made dangerous by the US army. When Bill returns from Slick's funeral in Oklahoma, he places the prayer sticks deep in the mine shaft where he works, humbly asking Slick to 'help us with our life here' (Ortiz 1992: 317), to watch over the men in the mine so that no one will be injured or killed as a result of the corporation's refusal to provide ample security to the workers. Bill's faith in the prayer sticks is an indication of his trust in the Native American beliefs. The following spring, Bill and Ida plant the corn in their garden, smiling as they think that Slick is helping them 'hold up/ the roof of Section 17' (Ortiz 1992: 317) and break up 'that clay dirt too' (Ortiz 1992: 317). The couple who lived in New Mexico with an unviable garden show enough confidence in planting corn in their garden, in the fond hope that it will sustain their lives in the new place.

Ortiz, through Slick's death and Bill's insight, illustrates that the same economic, social and political forces that destroy Indian communities will destroy the poor, the working class, and the 'white middle class' if they refuse to arrive at a concrete understanding of 'what Aacqu and her sister Pueblos in the Southwest are fighting for when they seek time and time again to bring attention to their struggle for land, water, and human rights' (Ortiz 1992: 360–1). At Slick's funeral, Bill's relatives claim that Slick has 'done his duty for America' (Ortiz 1992: 315), that he sacrificed his life to keep the world safe for democracy. Bill realizes that Slick did not die for democracy. He died because he was poor, and he needed a job to pay for his motorcycle, and his economic need led him to a dangerous place where he accidently stepped on a US landmine. 'By juxtaposing Bill and Ida's garden with a minefield in Vietnam and the equally dangerous Kerr-McGee mine shafts, Ortiz confronts the abstract ethics that serve to explain and justify state and corporate oppression of nature and "Others"' (Adamson 2001: 65). But Bill's work and friendship with Pete in the uranium mine, run by those whose aim is both profit and global nuclear domination, gives him insight into the connections between the linked oppression of nature and Others in both the United States and Vietnam.

In 'To Change In a Good Way', as a result of his interactions with Pete and Mary, Bill acknowledges that 'us Okies maybe/have been wrong sometimes' (Ortiz 1992: 317). This poem sets the stage for an understanding between the Native Americans and other racial communities. Pete and Mary are the first Indians that he'd (Bill) ever known. He had grown up with the notion that his 'past folks' (Ortiz 1992: 315) had lived a hard life 'fighting off Indians to build homes/on new land so we (they)could live the way/we (they)are right now advanced and safe/from peril' (Ortiz 1992: 315). Bill becomes a transformed person due to his friendship with Pete which reiterates the significance of the title 'To Change In a Good Way'. He takes onus of his own and his people's intentional and unintentional acts of oppression towards nature and others, thus, rejecting his former narrow and socially-constructed attitudes about people of other races, species that are not human, and lands that are considered fallen. For the first time, he begins to understand the broader social, economic, and political forces that connect him more closely to people like Pete than to those who gain profit by destroying natural resources and exploiting economically disadvantaged people in unjust wars or unsafe mines. It also begins the process of healing for Bill's grief and hurt as a result of Slick's death.

Simon Ortiz does not indulge in nature-writing merely to draw attention to environmental problems in the simple hope of raising individual consciousness which might then lead to a wholesome political change. Neither does he romanticize nature. Instead it is a nature-writing which emphasizes the plight of the people and the land affected by ruthless corporatization. His environmental praxis is in reminding that the people of Deetseyamah are still drinking water contaminated by the uranium-processing mills that closed in the 1980s when the market for uranium waned out, and that there still remains a toxic presence in the community. It is literature that rests its hope in organized community resistance to social and environmental justice. Simon Ortiz's work brings people of varied races and classes together in the pages of his writing and unites issues as variant as work place safety and sustainable agriculture, toxic sites and hallowed shrines, depleted aquifers and community health, economic development and wilderness protection. His poems are songs of hope, songs that imagine people might 'change things in a good way'.

Simon Ortiz, through his highly accessible narrative voice, thus tells the story of his Acoma Pueblo heritage and culture, and keeps the memory of the Acoma's experiences with the white civilization alive. In *Fight Back*, Ortiz truly is fighting back against oppression, colonization, exploitation, and technological progress that is blind, destructive and dehumanizing. By relaying these stories, Ortiz contextualizes American capitalist injustice and hypocrisy in order to set the stage for change, which begins with redefining the idea of progress. For Ortiz, progress is not determined by technological progress alone. If technological advancement leads to depleting of natural resources regardless of the people who live in that territory, then that progress is futile. If technology leaves lasting damage and does not create positive change then it is certainly not in the interest of humanity. In the interview with Kathleen Manley and Paul W. Rae, Ortiz asserts that if technology goes against being human, then we have to fight and resist it, and pursue a creative relationship with technology in order to avoid becoming complacently dependent upon it (Manley & Rea 1989: 371). Just as the deep ecologists, Ortiz believes that, that which goes against being human alienates people from each other and themselves as well as from the non-human natural world.

References

Adamson, Joni, *American Indian Literature, Environmental Justice, and Ecocriticism: The Middle Passage,* Tucson: The University of Arizona Press, 2001.

Allen, Paula Gunn, 'The Sacred Hoop: A Contemporary Perspective', *The Sacred Hoop: Recovering the Feminine in American Indian Traditions*, Boston: Beacon, 1986.

Carlisle, Rodney P., *Manifest Destiny and the Expansion of America,* California: ABC-CLIO Inc, 2007.

Chavis, Benjamin, 'Foreword', in *Confronting Environmental Racism: Voices from the Grassroots,* ed. Robert D. Bullard, Boston: South End Press, 1993.

Cronon, William, *Changes in the Land: Indians, Colonists, and the Ecology of New England,* New York: Hill and Wang, 1983.

Di Chiro, G.D., 'Nature as Community: The Convergence of Environment and Social Justice', in *The Struggle for Environmental Democracy: Environmental Justice Movements in the United States,* ed. Daniel Faber, New York: Guilford, 1998.

Dobson, John M., *Belligerence, Brinkmanship, and the Big Stick: A Historical Encyclopedia of American Diplomatic Concepts,* California: ABC-CLIO, 2009

Dreese, Donelle N., *Ecocriticism, Creating Self and Place in Environmental and American Indian Literatures,* New York: Peter Lang Publishing Inc, 2002.

Fox, Warwick, 'The Deep Ecology-Ecofeminism Debate and its Parallels', in *Deep Ecology for the Twenty-First Century*, ed. George Sessions, Boston and London: Shambhala Publications, Inc, 1995.

Frail, T.A., 'Top 10 Unforgettable Editorials', Smithsonian.com, 15 March 2011, accessed on 31 July 2015.

Garrard, Greg, *Ecocriticism (The New Critical Idiom)*, repr., London and New York: Routledge, 2007.

Hale, Lorraine, *Native American Education: A Reference Handbook*, California: ABC-CLIO, 2002.

Krupat, Arnold, *Ethnocriticism*, Berkeley: University of California Press, 1992.

Lincoln, Kenneth, 'Blue Medicine', in *Leslie Marmon Silko's Ceremony: A Casebook,* ed. Allan Richard Chavkin, New York: Oxford University Press Inc, 2002.

Lundquist, Suzanne, *Native American Literatures: An Introduction*, New York: Continuum, 2004.

Manley, Kathleen and Paul W. Rea, 'An Interview with Simon Ortiz', *Journal of the Southwest*, vol. 31, no. 2, Autumn 1989.

Ortiz, Simon, *Woven Stone,* Tucson: University of Arizona Press, 1992.

Platt, Kamala. 'Ecocritical Chicana Literature: Ana Castillo's, "Virtual Realism"', *Interdisciplinary Studies in Literature and Environment*, vol. 3, no. 1, Summer 1996.

Schweninger, Lee, 'Writing Nature: Silko and Native Americans as Nature Writers', *Multi-Ethnic Literature of the United States*, vol. 18, no. 2, 1993.

Swann, Brian, 'Introduction: Only the Beginning', in *Harper's Anthology of 20th Century Native American Poetry,* ed. Niatum, Duane, San Francisco: Harper San Francisco, 1988.

Editor and Contributors

SHIVANI JHA is Assistant Professor, Bharati College, University of Delhi. She specializes in the field of Ecocriticism and has presented papers in several national and international seminars. Apart from environmental studies, her areas of interest are feminism, romanticism and Indian writing in English. She is the author of *Ecocritical Readings: Rethinking Nature and Environment* (2015).

RAMBHAU M. BADODE is Professor of English, University of Mumbai. He is also Director, Garware Institute of Career Education and Development, University of Mumbai, since 2011; and Director, Confucius Institute, University of Mumbai, since 2013. His areas of specialization include modern British fiction, American fiction and African-American women's fiction, literature written in English and in Translation, and contemporary literary theories. He is the author of *The Novels of Doris Lessing: Catastrophe and Survival* (2004).

BINI B.S. is a Post-Doctoral Fellow at Balvant Parekh Centre for General Semantics and Other Human Sciences, Baroda. She is also one of the editors of *Anekaant: A Journal of Polysemic Thought* and the Managing Editor of *The Journal of Contemporary Thought*.

RASHMI LEE GEORGE is Assistant Professor, Department of English, St. Xavier's College, Mumbai. Broadly, her areas of research interest include postcolonial literature, Ecocriticism and Native American literature. Currently, she is working on her Doctoral thesis on Native American fiction from 1990 onwards.

NEENU KUMAR is teaching at Department of English, Aditi Mahavidyalaya, University of Delhi. She has several articles to her credit in books and journals. Her project on 'Locating Women in the Context of Partition: An Account of Lived Experiences and Unheard Voices' has been produced as a documentary.

NISHA TIWARI is Assistant Professor, Department of English, Bharati College, University of Delhi. Her research and teaching interests include gender and sexuality studies as well as literary and culture studies. She has contributed a wide range of publications and papers in the aforementioned areas of study.

Index